I0033569

BUSINESS WRITING, PERIOD.

a no-sweat, no-stress guide
to getting your ideas on paper

by K. T. Maclay

SkateKey Productions
New York, New York

© COPYRIGHT 2006 BY K. T. MACLAY, ALL RIGHTS RESERVED.

No part of this book may be reproduced in any form, by photostat, microfilm, xerography, or any other means, or incorporated into any information retrieval system, electronic or mechanical, without the written permission of the copyright owner.

PRINTED IN THE UNITED STATES OF AMERICA

ISBN 0-9786435-6-9

Cover design: John Morris-Reihl www.artntech.com

CONTENTS

WARNING

This is a counter-intuitive book. It will tell you to do things that fly in the face of most things you've been told about writing. It will make suggestions that sound improbable, but that will make the *process* of writing easier than you ever dreamed it could be.

Those who profit from this book are writers who are willing to:

♦ suspend their disbelief

♦ look and sound imperfect on paper

♦ take chances

♦ enjoy writing.

ALL OTHERS SHOULD PROCEED WITH CAUTION

CHAPTER 1: PUTTING IT OFF VS. GETTING IT OVER WITH

The "I-Don't-Wanna-Write" Syndrome. Some people call it "procrastination." It's the first hurdle to clear before beginning to write. All of us procrastinate, not that it helps. What interests me is that so few of us realize (1) that we worry a great deal, and (2) exactly what it is that we worry about. So it is with procrastination. It took me years to realize that by calling what I was doing "research," I had merely given procrastination another name. Whatever I called it, it never got the writing done any quicker. If knowledge is power, then knowing that I'm putting things off will help me get down to doing them sooner rather than later. To find out your own procrastination pattern, please take this quiz:

PROCRASTINATION GUILT INDEX (PGI)

Activity	Time Spent	Excuse	Personal Guilt Level
			1=not guilty 10=very guilty
Research Go to library Talk to experts Read pertinent material	120 hours	Need information	1 2 3 4 5 6 7 8 9 10
Coffee Get up Go to kitchen Make coffee Drink coffee Wash cup	3 hours (add 5 hours if you go out for coffee with friends)	Need energy Need a break	1 2 3 4 5 6 7 8 9 10

Paper or Magazine	2.5 hours	Need a break	1 2 3 4 5 6 7 8 9 10

Go to another room
Read everything, including real
estate ads

Format Project	1.75 hours	Needs to look professional	1 2 3 4 5 6 7 8 9 10

Try lots of different fonts
Add and remove graphics
Adjust and readjust tables

Phone a Friend

Go through address book	6.5 hours	Project isn't going well	1 2 3 4 5 6 7 8 9 10

Find friend who can talk on
phone.
Complain about being late with
document.

Add up all the numbers you've circled and write your total here:

Total Personal Guilt Index: _____

The bad news: If you even bothered *to take* the test you have a problem with procrastination

The good news: You're just like the rest of us.

Your Total Personal Guilt Index will tell you how much procrastination contributes to your battle with writer's block. The guiltier you are, the higher your score the more trouble you'll have getting started. Not to worry. We'll explore removing the trauma of getting started in Chapter 2.

JOURNALS

Now, I'd like you to **start a separate file, or keep a separate notebook** for your journals.

After each chapter, pause a minute, or an hour, or even several hours, to let the material sink in. Then open your journal, write the chapter heading at the top of the page and answer these three questions:

- What happened while you were working with the material in the chapter—were there any new ideas or insights into your own work that popped up?

- How did you feel about the work you did in the chapter?

- What do you want to do with the information you've practiced in the chapter?

The questions will be the same for each chapter. The answers will be different, of course, but so will your insights and attitudes. Keeping journals is essential practice for people who want to write better than they do now. Journals also give you a personal record of your progress in this course.

Please write your journal entry for Chapter 1. Do it **NOW. I mean this! You'll get more from this book if you do the exercises immediately instead of waiting for later...so when you see "Do it NOW" do it—***NOW.*

Your Notes Here

CHAPTER 2: GETTING STARTED

No matter what you're writing (letters, reports, e-mails, memos, proposals, complaints, thank you's, commendations) the first step is starting. It's easier than you think, but to do it *immediately* and *effectively* there are certain things it helps to know: what writing is; where writing comes from; where *ideas* come from; how to think and write at the same time; why your left brain and your right brain work differently; how the connection between procrastination, perfectionism and paralysis holds you up, wastes your time and makes you uncomfortable. Whew!

This Chapter will show you how to start and explain why starting *quickly* saves time, stress and misery.

Contrary to what you learned in the academic world, writing is not painful, torturous, backbreaking work. It doesn't have to do with "impressive" or complicated sentences. It's not even something you have to think about very hard. I know this is irreverent, but trust me, writing is as easy as talking—when you know how to do it.

So, let's look at some of the reasons you might think writing is hard. This is your chance to turn those old ideas around so you don't sit down at your screen with five strikes against you. Here are five reasons you may be having a difficult time writing:

Reason #1: **Your sixth grade teacher was a perfectionist.**

She insisted on perfect spelling, perfect organization and perfect punctuation from the minute your pen hit the paper. There were no cross-outs allowed. Your handwriting had to be neat and you had to stick in all the difficult vocabulary words you covered in class that week.

CONCEPT #1:   *Your sixth grade teacher was WRONG.*

Reason # 2: **College texts said detailed outlines resulted in superior work.**

Good writers agree that good writing needs a plan, but forcing yourself to go from A to B to C (before warming up your brain) is counter productive. Trying to make a detailed list of your thoughts from the minute you sit down at your screen doesn't work. The reason is simple: the part of your brain that creates writing doesn't *ever* follow a logical order.

CONCEPT #2:   *Rigid outlines don't work.*

Reason #3: **You want to start with the perfect fact, word, phrase, or sentence.**

The problem here is how much time it takes to turn up the perfect word, fact, phrase or opening sentence. This is true of anyone—you, me or Shakespeare for that matter. Usually that perfect whatever-it-is turns up around paragraph three, but you have to be writing to find it. Most people start writing, stop, cross out, and then start again. In the old days, all this method was good for was creating a room full of crumpled paper. Now all it creates is a mostly blank screen. Waiting for the perfect beginning produces frustration, not writing. All "trying for perfection" does is cause trouble.

Write these concepts (three to five times each) on a separate page:

Concept #1	Concept #2	Concept #3
My sixth grade teacher was WRONG.	Rigid outlines don't work.	There is no perfect start.

Important Note: There are 57 "concepts" in this book. When you come to a concept, copy it (by hand) three to five times on a separate page. The more times you copy a concept, the easier that concept is to remember. You'll find the concepts coming back to you as you write. They'll help you get through difficult patches and remind you to do the right things.

CONCEPT #3:   *There is no perfect start.*

Reason #4: **You're convinced you're not up to the task.**

You may think you can't write that memo, e-mail, or quarterly report, but the fact is that your job depends on writing it.

Remember: Feelings aren't facts. No matter how not-up-to-the-task you may feel, you *are* up to taking a stab at it. The sign I have above my PC screen says, "Anything worth doing is worth doing badly." That sign has saved my life a hundred times because it always helps me get started.

CONCEPT #4:   *Anything worth doing is worth doing badly.*

Reason #5: **You're scared of what your reader(s) will think of your writing.**

Professional writers (the writers who work for money) are people who feel the fear and do it anyway. That's why there are so few professional writers. The one thing to remember about readers when you first approach a blank PC screen is that there *are* no readers. Not for a first draft, anyway. Your draft is for *your eyes only* until you polish it and send it out, and we're not up to that part yet.

CONCEPT #5:   *You're the **only** one who reads your first draft.*

Anybody who ever had to write anything has used reasons #1 through #5 to avoid putting pen to paper or fingers to keyboard. We've *all* wanted to be perfect right from the git-go. At the very beginning of anything you want to put on paper, perfection is not your friend. In the beginning, wanting to be perfect is the specter casting a shadow on your work. Ignore it or snap your fingers and make it go away, otherwise, it will lead you to stare at a blank PC screen and weep.

CONCEPT #6:   *Perfection is not your friend.*

Write these concepts (three to five times each) on a separate page:

Concept #4	Concept #5	Concept #6
Anything worth doing is worth doing badly.	I'm the only one who reads my first draft.	Perfection is not my friend.

Writing is thinking on paper. If you can think in your head, if you can think as you speak, you should be able to think on paper. There are differences, but there *is* one important similarity: when you think in your head and when you think as you speak, your thoughts don't always align themselves in a logical order. They are seldom neat. They frequently go off on tangents. Some thoughts are just fragments and you expect others to know what you mean and how you'd finish the thought. Sometimes your thoughts work well; sometimes they don't work at all.

The same random thought process governs getting ideas down on paper. The trouble is, most of us think we need to have all our ducks marching in an orderly file at all times. We also think we need to be precise in our explanations on paper. The ducks-in-a-row theory would be fine if it worked, but it doesn't. The truth is that "writing-thought" is just as chaotic as "thinking-thought" or "speaking-thought." All writing comes from the place in your brain that doesn't give a hoot about logical order. It's a fast, sloppy, uncontrollable place and sometimes it turns words into gibberish. Or, it takes a dogleg to the left. Or it goes in circles. Or, it repeats itself. This chaos is good if you can get it down on paper. Let me repeat that, chaos is good. Sloppiness is part of the writing process—an invaluable part. You can't afford to ignore it.

CONCEPT #7:   *Chaos is good*

Imagine you're sitting at a blank screen starting a report on the reasons your department needs to reorganize. You have lots of ideas floating around in your brain. Some ideas are louder than others. Some are whispering. Some are just jumping around trying to get your attention.

You know what you do first. Like most people, you probably try to quiet all those ideas. To start at the beginning. To make a logical outline. To cover everything in A to Z order. To do it "right." (Those demon reasons are still coming up!) Many people think that this method will save them time. What it really does is kill those unruly ideas. The screen stays blank. The writer feels an urgent need to go to the kitchen for an egg salad sandwich. The work sits there or gets pushed off to the side of the desk so the writer can do something easier, like a shopping list. The pressure mounts. The work becomes a heavy weight. The deadline passes. The guilt piles up and the writer, instead of basking in the warm glow of *having written* something, is still under the curse of *having to write* something.

To understand this dilemma, we're going inside your brain for a moment. The dynamics of how your brain functions govern the way you write and explain why writing works when approached *one* way and doesn't work when approached *another*.

Your brain has a left and a right hemisphere. The left hemisphere handles the verbal, linear, logical, mathematical, precise stuff. It automatically goes from A to B to C and on down the line in order. Your right hemisphere is disorderly, visual, creative, flight-prone, cunning and emotional. It sees or senses the big picture. It digresses. It captures the overview without bothering itself too much about the specifics. It's fast and not at all worried that it's not moving from point to point in order.

CONCEPT #8:   *Writing and editing are two different things.*

Write these concepts (three to five times each) on a separate page:

Concept #7	Concept #8	Concept #9
Chaos is good.	Writing and editing are two different things.	Start anywhere.

Inspiration ("*writing*") comes from your brain's right hemisphere. Organization ("*editing*") comes from its left hemisphere. The problem most people have with writing is that they try to work with both hemispheres at once. Writing is one thing. Editing is something completely different. If you try to write and edit at the same time, the editing process (left hemisphere) cancels out the writing process (right hemisphere) and there you are again—you and your blank screen.

Writer's block is a classic example of ignoring right brain chaos and trying to tap into left brain order prematurely.

CONCEPT #9:   *Start anywhere.*

All writers need to do two things at the beginning of any project: *start anywhere* and *fill the page*. That's all. Take all that boisterous stuff in your mind and get it down on paper. Allow it to be foolish. Forget punctuation spelling and grammar. Just fill the page as fast as you can. Let anything on your mind come out through your fingertips. If your mind is blank, write: *"My mind is blank...I can't think of anything to say here...I wish I were in Fiji...Why did I sign up for this course...I'm completely stuck here...There is nothing to write...I want to go home... Why did I think I had anything to say on this subject? "*

Write whatever you like but keep your hands moving on the keyboard. Why? Because there is a kinetic connection between moving your hands and keeping your brain awake. Go for speed. Don't worry about corrections. Never look back.

CONCEPT #10:   *The faster you write, the more you see.*

The ideas are in there; trust me. But the only way they'll feel free enough to come out and play on the paper is if your hands are moving. The minute you stop to think, your ideas go off to the water cooler and may never come back. The more you move, the more ideas you generate. I'm not saying the ideas are all *good* ones. What I *am* saying is that there are definitely *some* good ideas and *some* excellent ones roaming around in your head and they're only valuable if they're on paper so you can work with them. Here, you're thinking and writing at the same time. The thing you're *not* doing is trying to shove anything into order. And that's the important point.

CONCEPT #11:   *Just fill the page*

The way to start writing immediately and painlessly is to suspend the judgment of your left brain and let your right brain have a field day. Give it all the space and freedom it needs. When your right brain has said everything it wants to say, take a deep breath. Print out what you've written and then, and *only* then, let the left brain take over.

Write these concepts (three to five times each) on a separate page:

Concept #10	Concept #11	Concept #12
The faster I write the more I see.	Just fill the page.	Have fun.

CONCEPT #12:   *Have fun.*

If there's fun in writing, SpeedWriting the first draft is where you'll find it. SpeedWriting is a speedy, uncensored way to get your ideas down on paper. For your first brush with SpeedWriting you'll want to follow the rules. You'll find them below.

SPEEDWRITING RULES

1.   **Write as quickly as you can.**

     Keep your hand(s) moving. Hand motion is the direct route to the creativity centers in your brain. Whatever happens, keep your hand(s) moving forward.

2.   **Keep writing. Don't stop to think.**

     This is very important. Stopping for any reason works against you. It gets in the way of the *real* thinking you're doing as you write.

3.   **Write whatever is in your head— no matter how irrelevant or silly it seems.**

     "A stick, a stone, a hat, a bump" may be irrelevant elsewhere, but here they're the preamble to some very good ideas.

4. **If your mind goes blank—write anything.**

Write: "My mind is blank." or, "This is stupid." Write your name, or my name. Write nonsense words. Write "Twas brillig, and the slithy toves," but just keep writing.

5. **Avoid backspacing, correcting, deleting or crossing out.**

Just keep moving forward. Stopping is a difficult habit to break, but refusing to stop for any reason is worth the trouble.

6. **Write for five minutes, then stop writing.**

Write without stopping. Then stop writing, take a deep breath, and exhale. I mean it. It's important to get into the habit of breathing every time you write. You'd be surprised how many of us stop breathing all together once our hands hit the keyboard. Watch yourself next time you write and see what your pattern is.

Your right brain loves filling the page. Your left brain adores cutting unnecessary stuff. It thrives on linear flow. It revels in clarifying murky thoughts. Given the raw material (your right brain product) to work with, your left brain can do wonders, quickly. And that's the watchword: "quickly." No more procrastinating, no more seeking perfection, no more pain, no more stress. Just let each brain hemisphere work the way it wants to—and before you know it, you have a rough draft. The SpeedWriting Exercise that follows will give you the feeling of writing anything on any topic quickly and easily.

Do the SpeedWriting Exercise (below) **NOW.**

SPEEDWRITING EXERCISE

The best way to fill the page without making yourself miserable is to SpeedWrite. There are many names for this method, but the mechanics are always the same. Open a blank document. Write anything that comes into your mind about your topic. Write through the blank spots. Write just to fill the page. Keep your hands moving.

In this case, let's say the topic is "Where I'll be five years from now." Write in the present tense, i.e. *"I'm on the terrace of my villa in Marbella. The butler brings me an icy lemonade and tells me that the car is ready for my trip into town."* Or, " *I'm a wealthy brain surgeon who travels all over the world to operate on the most difficult cases. Today I'm catching a flight from Toronto to Uzbekistan to...."* Write anything. Don't stop to "think"–just keep your fingers moving over the keys. Don't edit or correct. Don't worry about spelling. Just keep writing.

If your mind goes blank, *keep writing anyway*. It doesn't matter what you write. You can write your name, or my name, or *"I hate this exercise"* or *"I wonder if that new guy in Marketing is dating anyone."* Just *fill the page*. If you can't remember a word or a name, leave a blank space. Write as fast as you can for at least five minutes without stopping. Set the kitchen timer. I repeat: write without stopping, editing, correcting, worrying or looking back. At the end of five minutes, stop writing, take a deep breath and put the page aside.

CONCEPT #13:   *Brainstorming on paper makes for unexpected ideas.*

SPEEDWRITING QUICK QUIZ

Congratulations. You've filled the page. Now answer these questions:

- Was the SpeedWriting easy?   Yes   No
- Did it feel painful?   Yes   No
- Was it quick?   Yes   No
- Did the writing seem to take off by itself
  after a while?   Yes   No
- Did any new ideas come to you while you were
  writing?   Yes   No

- What were they? (Write them in the space below)

- ◆ Did the ideas appear after a few lines of nonsense?　　Yes　　No
- ◆ Where did your most important statement show up?

Beginning　　Middle　　End

- ◆ Was it in the first sentence?

Yes　　No

- ◆ If not, where was it? (Write your answer in the space below)

- ◆ Was it *easy* to fill the page?

Yes　　No

MORE SPEEDWRITING EXERCISES

SpeedWriting opens your mind to endless possibilities. The first time you try it, you'll see what I mean.

Keep each SpeedWritten piece in its *own notebook,* on its *own page,* or in its *own section* so you can come back and work on it later. Many writers have found the best time to SpeedWrite is when they first get up, before they even have their eyes completely open. Some people refer to this writing as "morning pages." They find if they SpeedWrite three or four pages each morning they have less resistance to getting started writing later in the day. You don't need a topic for morning pages. You can just ramble on and get all the stuff that's running around in your head down on paper. You'll be surprised at what you discover, and how free you feel to write later in the day. Don't read over what you've written. Morning pages are not for publication, they're for getting you warmed up.

If you need some topics to SpeedWrite about, try the ones I've suggested below. Set a timer. Work for five minutes then stop wherever you are. (Remember to follow the rules.)

SPEEDWRITING TOPICS

a.   Who am I?
b.   The most interesting character I've ever met
c.   The first time I made a deal, worked in an office, kissed a girl/boy
d.   What I'll be doing five years from today
e.   Communications
f.   Working conditions
g.   Overtime
h.   Salary/bonus
i.   Job description
j.   Status report

Write your journal for Chapter 2 **NOW.** See Page 7 for instructions.

YOUR NOTES HERE

CHAPTER 3: MINING YOUR IDEA BANKS

Since you're writing on the job, I assume you know something about your subject. If you look at the SpeedWriting you did in Chapter 2, you'll see that, mixed in with the cobwebby stuff, there are some solid ideas, perhaps even some *good* ideas.

In this Chapter we'll discover

- ◆ where your real ideas kick in
- ◆ how to find the good stuff
- ◆ how to separate the wheat from the chaff
- ◆ how to find *other* ideas
- ◆ how to create Bubble Diagrams
- ◆ how to use other ways to brainstorm new material

Take out the SpeedWriting Exercise you did in Chapter 1. Look at it carefully. Put a circle around your *best* idea. Were there any other *good* ideas in the SpeedWriting document? Circle them.

Where did the *good* ideas start to kick in? Paragraph one? Paragraph three? Somewhere near the end? Were there any *new* ideas that appeared during the writing? Did any aspect of this process surprise you? If so, *how* were you surprised and *what* were you surprised about?

SpeedWrite your experience with SpeedWriting in a separate document **NOW**.

Oddly enough, the best ideas seldom happen in paragraph one of your rough drafts. Paragraph one is like the stretching exercises you do before going out to jog. It's a warm up. It's a wake up call to your brain. It doesn't mean your brain's gotten out of bed yet. It may take your brain some time to open its eyes, to stretch, to get accustomed to being awake. So, by the time your brain actually gets its feet on the floor, you're somewhere around paragraph three.

If you keep writing, the good ideas will lead to other ideas, and the writing will take off by itself. When you're done you'll have a number of good ideas and quite a few other things. Circle the good ideas. Cross out the other things. Now, you're on your way.

CONCEPT #14: *Do one thing at a time.*

Look at the good ideas. Is there a message in these ideas? A theme? A suggestion of organization? Is there material you'd like to add? Material you'd like to throw out? Is there someone you'd like to call to check on a theory or a premise? Note down any new information on your draft. It doesn't have to look neat; this is a rough draft—remember, nobody sees it but you. You're now ready for the next step: Bubble Diagrams.

Write these concepts (three to five times each) on a separate page:

Concept #13	Concept #14	Concept #15
Brainstorming on paper makes for unexpected ideas.	Do one thing at a time.	Picture it.

What are Bubble Diagrams? Good that you've asked, because different people call them different things. Whatever you call them, Bubble Diagrams *literally* draw a picture of what's going on in your brain at any one time. They are a surprisingly painless way to generate ideas *and* limit your topic.

We've already talked about left and right brain activity, so let's talk about how people learn things. Basically, learners fall into four categories, or any combination of the four:

- kinetic — people who learn by *moving*
- aural — people who learn by *listening*
- visual — people who learn by *seeing*
- emotive — people who learn by *feeling*

No matter which category you fall into, SpeedWriting kickstarts your learning process. Your fingers are moving and you're hearing words with your inner ear. As you hear, your emotions will come into play.

Making Bubble Diagrams brings your *visual* powers into the mix. Adding this visual element often lets your brain to come up with ideas that are lurking below the surface.

BUBBLE DIAGRAMS

Let's say you have a basic idea of what you want to write, but you can't think of anything to support it. The first thing to do is find a large, blank sheet of paper, turn it *horizontally*, write your general topic in the middle of it and draw a circle around it, like this:

TRAINING SEMINAR

Your topic can be anything--"Staggered Work Hours," "Paternity Leave," "Reorganizing the Training Department" — but try to keep its description to one or two words. The topic I'm going to map out from my own notes, is: "American Letters Seminar."

Your next task is to write a word or two for each idea you have that relates to your topic. *Important*: write in a totally haphazard, random way. Use just a word or two for any idea. Use the whole page. Write diagonally. Vertically. Any which way. If you come upon a topic that has side issues, draw a circle around the topic and connect the side issues to that circle. I'll show you pictures in a minute.

My document (the one I'm going to illustrate for you) will eventually become a checklist for running a training seminar. At the moment it's just an idea, but as soon as I start writing down related ideas and connecting them to the main idea with lines, I start to think of other things I need to check on in order to run my event.

CONCEPT #15: *Picture it.*

The more I draw, the more I see. The more I see, the more I connect. The more I connect, the more I think of other topics relating to the ones I've just drawn. Here's my Bubble Diagram of the training seminar checklist:

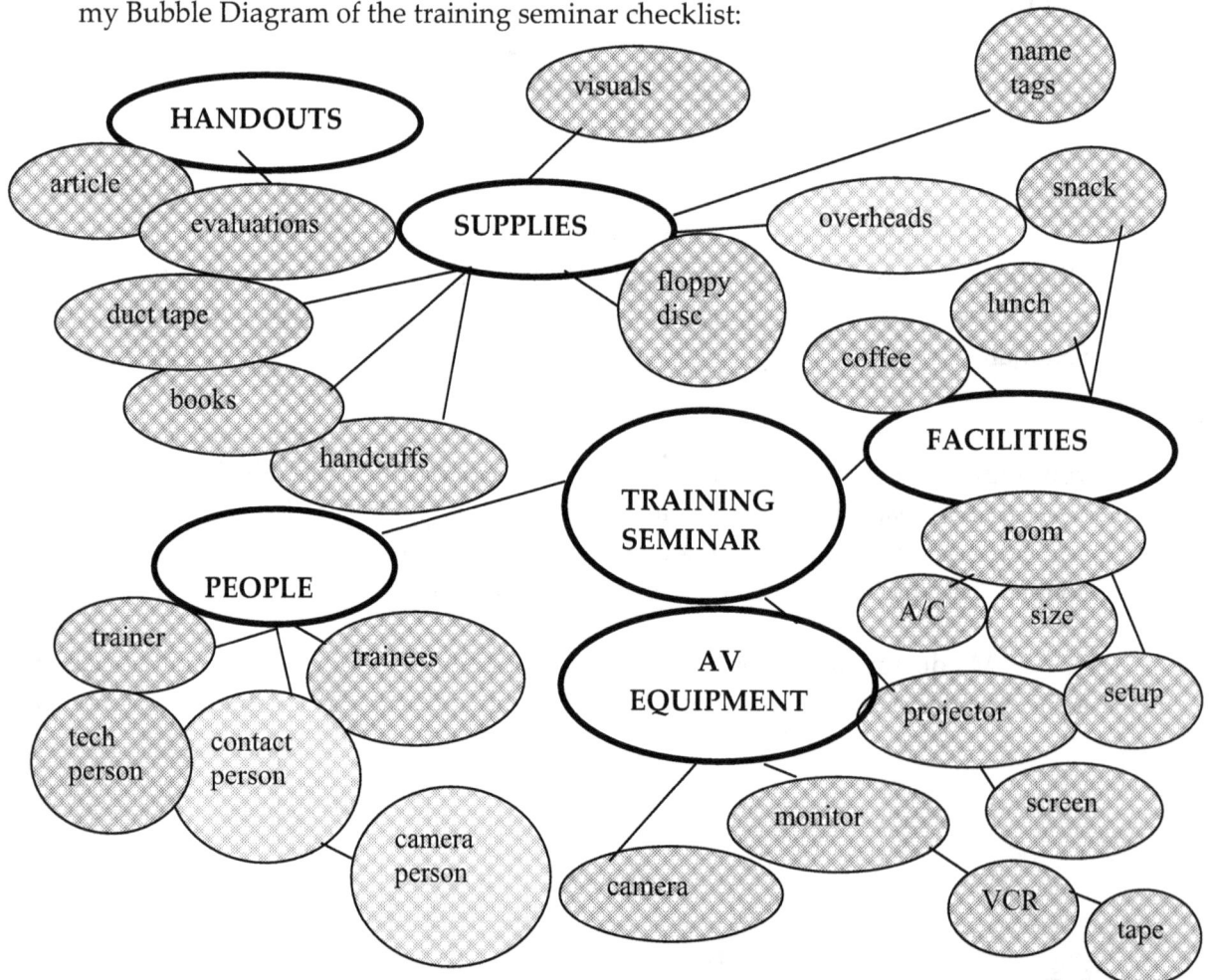

Note: My original bubble diagram didn't look as neat as the diagram on the previous page. Sloppy is okay here. Getting your ideas sorted out on paper is what counts.

Drawing Bubble Diagrams is like having a brainstorming meeting without having to coordinate with five other people and schedule a conference room. You can brainstorm any time, anywhere. It's easy. It's quick and it's efficient. Some people even find it fun.

Bubble Diagrams are an excellent way to bring up ideas that were floating around just below the surface of your consciousness. New things come to you as you make connections. You'll see. In my case the training seminar Bubble Diagram generated new questions and avenues of thought—most of them concerning things I was afraid I'd forget: Did I forget the camera person? Lunch? Coffee? The projector?

My advanced students tell me that Bubble Diagrams
are a great way to take notes (and stay awake)
at seminars or on conference calls.

BUBBLE DIAGRAMS: RECAP

1. Turn your blank page so it is horizontal.
2. Write your main idea (in a word or two) in the center of the page.
3. Draw a circle around your idea.
4. Look at the circled idea.
5. Jot down (in a word or two) any ideas that pop into your head that connect to the main idea.
6. Circle each of those ideas.
7. Draw a line connecting each of the new ideas to the main idea.
8. Look at each subordinate idea.
9. Repeat steps 5 and 6.
10. Draw lines connecting the new ideas to each subordinate idea.

Here's a Bubble Diagram I did for a public relations training manual project for an international cosmetics company:

BUBBLE DIAGRAM FOR PR MANUAL

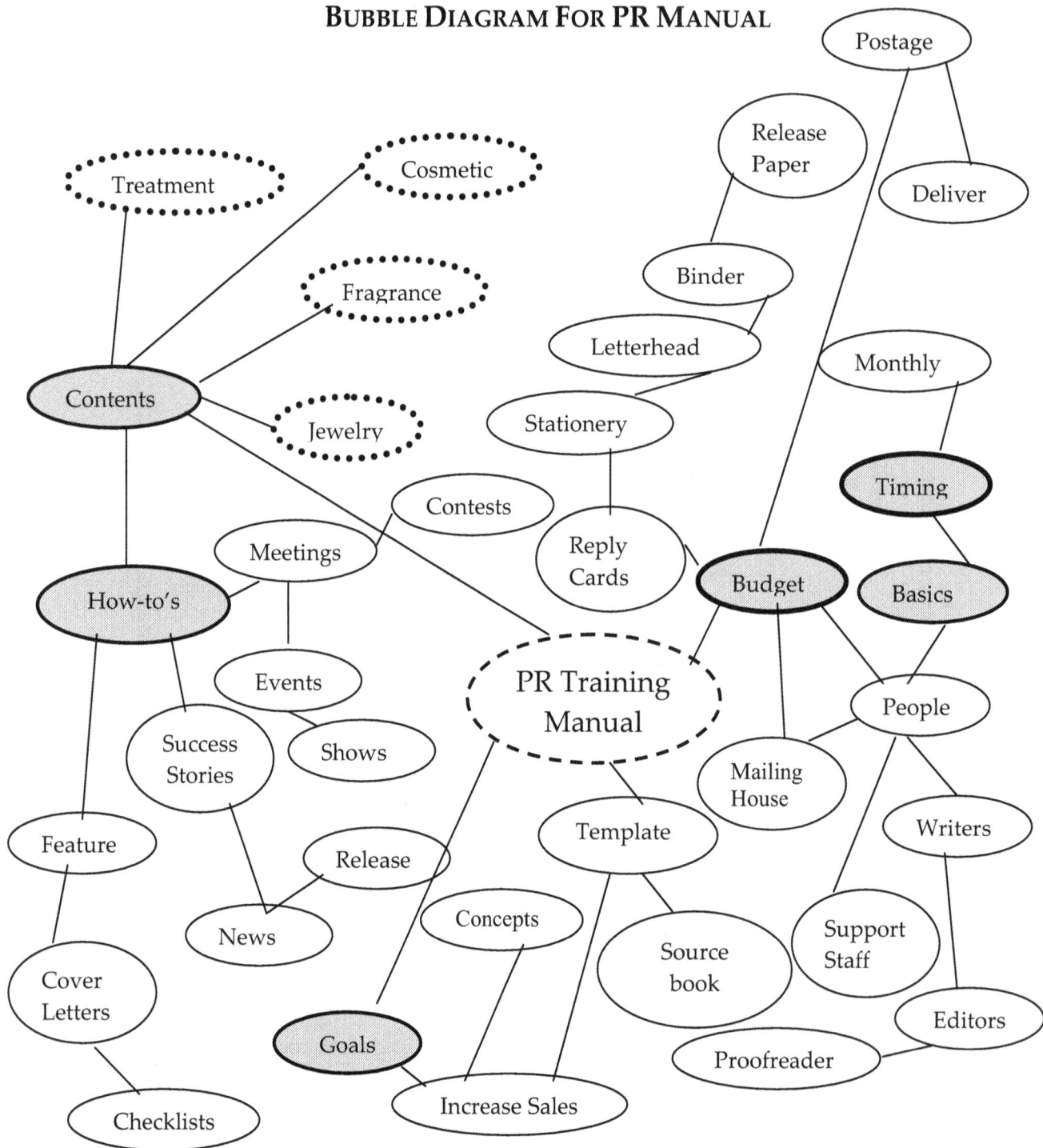

Postage

Release Paper

Deliver

Treatment

Cosmetic

Fragrance

Binder

Monthly

Letterhead

Contents

Jewelry

Stationery

Timing

Contests

Reply Cards

Budget

Basics

Meetings

How-to's

PR Training Manual

People

Events

Shows

Success Stories

Mailing House

Writers

Feature

Release

Template

Cover Letters

News

Concepts

Source book

Support Staff

Editors

Goals

Proofreader

Checklists

Increase Sales

Try drawing Bubble Diagrams on these topics:

a.	Tuition reimbursement	j.	Art
b.	Managers' meeting	k.	Music
c.	Office dress code	l.	Vacations
d.	New product intro	m.	Baseball
e.	Status report	n.	Golf
f.	Pitch letter	o.	Energy
g.	Invitation	p.	Moving
h.	Budget report	q.	Love
i.	Biographical information for company newsletter	r.	War

For some people, everything becomes clearer when they see a picture of the project. Other people find that they're more comfortable with Triangulation. The Triangle Method is especially handy when there are two sides to the issue: *pro and con, then and now, now and later.* Like making Bubble Diagrams, triangulation helps you see things graphically. It helps you remember things you would otherwise have forgotten. It brings up new ideas.

Turn to the next page to see how triangulation helped me map out an on-the-job training program for salespeople.

TRIANGULATION: ON-THE-JOB TRAINING FOR SALESPEOPLE

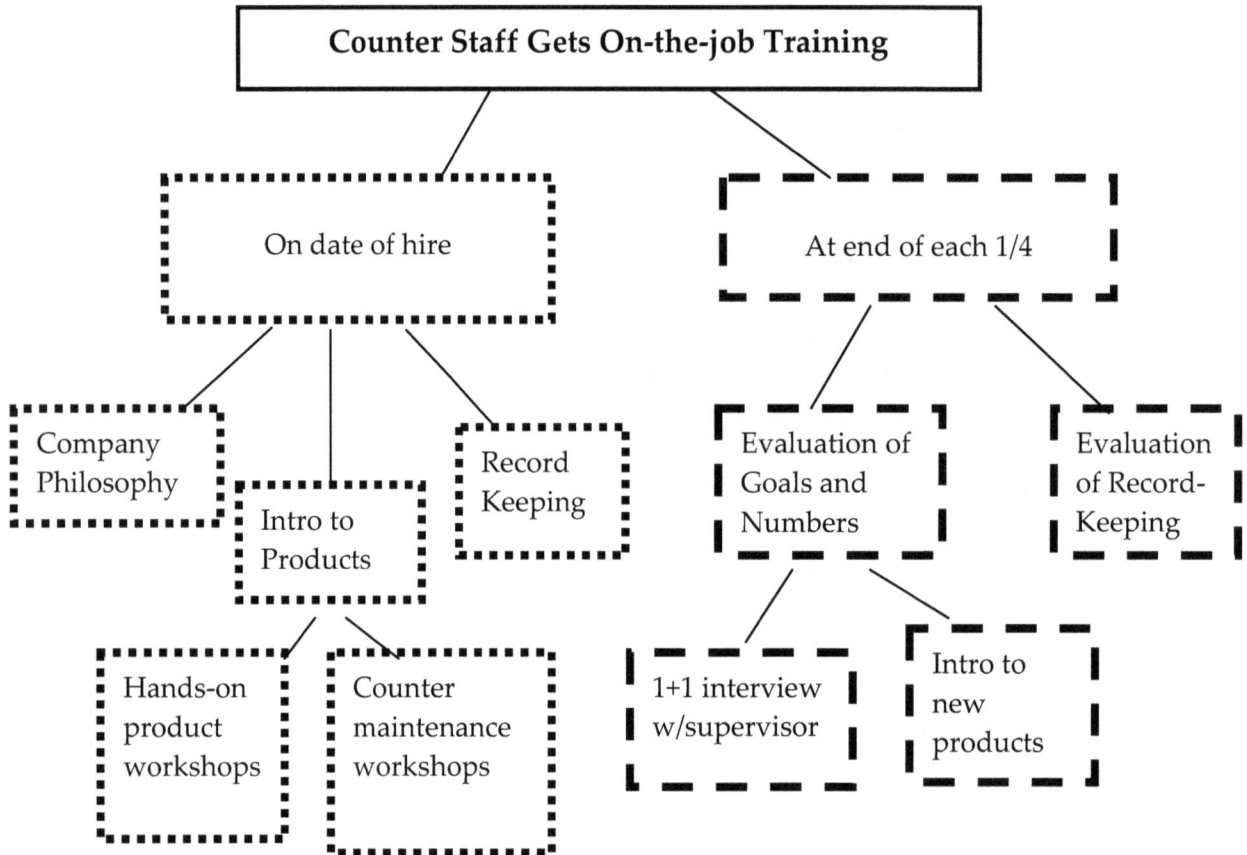

```
┌─────────────────────────────────────────────┐
│      Counter Staff Gets On-the-job Training   │
└─────────────────────────────────────────────┘
```

On date of hire

At end of each 1/4

Company Philosophy

Intro to Products

Record Keeping

Evaluation of Goals and Numbers

Evaluation of Record-Keeping

Hands-on product workshops

Counter maintenance workshops

1+1 interview w/supervisor

Intro to new products

INDEX CARD METHOD

I find the Index Card Method easiest to use when I have a long report or a complicated memo or speech to write. You'll need a pack of 3" x 5" blank index cards and a felt-tip pen. Like drawing Bubble Diagrams, the index card method uses one or two words to describe an idea, an example, or an illustration of that idea. Write one idea on each card as the idea occurs to you. Use single words or phrases. Once you have all your ideas down, lay the cards out on a big table (I've also used my bed or the floor) and arrange them to tell the story the way you want it told.

All three methods, Bubble Diagrams and Triangulation and Index Cards, plus SpeedWriting, are essential parts of jump-starting the writing process. The writing process itself is like making soup. You start with water and add a little bit of this and a little bit of that and eventually it becomes soup. At this stage in the writing process it hasn't become soup yet and you're still hauling spices down off the shelf. Don't worry. It will become soup eventually.

CONCEPT #16:   *It's not soup yet.*

"Yes, yes," you say — "But now I've spent all this time fooling around and I haven't done any writing yet." Ah — since writing is a form of thought — you've been writing all along without realizing it.

You'll notice that we haven't put anything formal on paper yet. This is *not* an oversight. Once you start typing anything that looks like a final piece of work, that work *seems* like it's written in stone. It may not be, but psychologically it's more difficult to change, rearrange, cut, or improve something that looks like it's already in print. It's better to have all the ingredients in front of you: your SpeedWriting, Bubble Diagram and any additional notes and/or figures you feel you need. The ingredients are always more flexible and easier to work with than a neatly- typed outline.

Oh, and about the time it takes to generate new ideas — once you practice doing it — it's about ten times faster (and much less painful) than staring at the screen. Better yet, it produces tangible results that will make your final document better.

CONCEPT #17:   *Practice makes better.*

> **Practice doesn't make perfect. At this stage, nothing is perfect.**

Write these concepts (three to five times each) on a separate page:

Concept #16	Concept #17	Concept #18
It's not soup yet.	Practice makes better.	Dialogue don't monologue.

Please write your journal entry for Chapter 3 **NOW.** See Page 7 for instructions.

YOUR NOTES HERE

CHAPTER 4: TALKING TO *ME*?

The difference between monologue and dialogue is: in a dialogue, you're talking to another human being and they're responding to you. That's communication—talking and listening, taking in your audience's concerns and responding to them. Good writing is just a *dialogue* with your readers.

If you are only saying what *you* want to say, you are conducting a *monologue*. Unless you're Hamlet, monologues in writing make your audience want to run out of the room screaming.

In person, it's easy to know your audience. They're right there in front of you responding to what you say and reacting to you. But on paper—you have no face-to-face contact, so it's vital to know as much about the person (people) you're writing for as possible

Once you know specifically who your audience is, you need to know some important things about them:

> *their* attitude about your topic
> how much *they* already know
> *their* questions

In this Chapter, we'll explore:

- ◆ getting to know your audience
- ◆ getting your audience's facts down on paper
- ◆ shifting to your audience's point of view

The trouble with most business writing today is *selfishness*. That's right, selfishness. It took me a long time to learn that writing is a *humble* activity. It wasn't a matter of what *I* wanted to tell people, it was a matter of what those people needed or *wanted* to know.

In my early days in the working world, I used to start all my memos with as much background material as I could muster. It never occurred to me that in order to be interested in the background material, readers were going to have to know *why* I was going on at such length to tell them about it. Did I want them to *do* something? Was I going to tell them how we could *save money* by approaching a problem from a new angle? Was I suggesting a *staff change*?

You get my drift. I was more concerned with *telling the whole story* from A to Z than I was with what my reader *really* wanted to know. Consequently, much of my correspondence wound up in that big yellowing paper pile that never gets looked at. Or, it got tossed out immediately without being read.

It also took me years to find out the only way to get my mail read was to *have a dialogue* with my reader. Most business writers don't even think about who's going to read what they're writing, or what that reader needs to *do* with the information.

CONCEPT #18:   *Dialogue, don't monologue.*

My cousin Berta calls frequently to tell me about her medical and financial conditions. She goes on at length. I have no idea what she wants from me. She never takes a breath, so I don't even get a chance to ask. I know she doesn't want my advice. All she really wants to do is talk. Every time I get one of these calls, I *stop listening* as soon as I find out who's on the phone.

Why am I telling you this? Because selfish writers talk to their readers with exactly the same concern Berta shows for me. Readers feel the writer's lack of interest in them. Readers respond appropriately — by tuning out.

CONCEPT #19:   *Resist the urge to tell the whole story.*

Making readers slog through unnecessary information before getting to the point wastes millions of hours and billions of business dollars. That time (and money) would be saved if writers only *thought of their readers* before sitting down at the keyboard. Thinking about readers would reduce an incomprehensible three-page document to a crisp one-paragraph message, or, even better, to a phone call. It would save trees in the forests. It would save birds and bees and little furry things in the woods. But, I digress. The thing to do to save all this wasted time, money and effort is to *put your readers' interests first.*

To avoid suffering an overdose of e-mail strings, try addressing each point in the original e-message *on* the original copy. Use a contrasting color ink for your response. Put your name and color key at the beginning of the original e-message.

Write these concepts (three to five times each) on a separate page:

Concept #19	Concept #20	Concept #21
Resist the urge to tell the whole story.	Know what I want from my reader.	Use active verbs.

THE EASY WAY TO PUT READERS INTERESTS FIRST

Ask yourself these questions:

Question 1: *Who am I writing for*? Okay, okay: *for whom am I writing*?

Am I writing for a manager who wants details about procedure? A boss who only wants to read about the big picture and hates detail? A tech department that needs to know *both* the "why" and the "how" of what I'm writing about?

Question 2:   *How much do my readers already know about the subject?*

Are they experts? Are they trainees? Are they laypeople? If I'm writing to people familiar with the terminology in my field, I can use that terminology freely. If I'm in retail, for example, and everyone I'm writing to knows that SKU stands for Stock Keeping Unit, fine. If the readers are *not* familiar with industry terminology, I need to make that terminology clear and simple for them.

Question 3:   *Do the readers already have objections to what I'm proposing?*

Is there one reader, or are there lots of readers? Do they all share the same problems and/or interests? Are there secondary readers—e.g., my manager reads my document and passes it along to my department head who passes it along to the CEO? Do any of my readers oppose my suggestions? If so, why?

The more I know about my readers, the better I'll be able to focus my document. The less I'll wander off into the thorny forest of extraneous detail. The less I'll find myself being too windy, or too brief.

Question 4:   *Do my readers know what I want from them?*

The only way to *get* what I want is to *know* what I want in the first place. Then say (or write) it as clearly as possible.

CONCEPT #20:   *Know what you want from your reader.*

Judging from the business letters and memos I get in the mail, most writers have no idea what they want me to do after reading what they've sent me. As a writer, not knowing what you want the reader to do for you is like putting a milk bucket under a bull—useless. So, 90 % of the time, if you don't tell the reader what you want them to do, your whole reason for writing is wasted. The quickest and easiest way to find out exactly what you want *before* you start writing is to find out what you want the **result** of your document to be. To find that result, all you have to do is complete the sentence:

"My reader will read this and will..."

Be careful about finishing this sentence with verbs like *"know"* or *"learn."* As in *"My reader will read this and will **know** more about the importance of estate planning"* or *"My reader will read this and will **learn** exactly what the Alumni fund is doing for Hodgepodge U."*

Since "know" and "learn" are *not* active verbs, they make it easy to slip into monologue mode and unlikely to get you the active result you want. Finding the right result helps focus your material and gets rid of anything that doesn't get you to that result quickly.

CONCEPT #21:   *When you want people to act, use active verbs.*

When I ask you to use "active" verbs I mean for you to come up with a result that looks something like one of the following examples:

- *sign* off on this artwork
- *approve* my proposal
- *pass along* my suggestions to management
- *give* me a raise
- *fund* my program
- *hire* a nurse for the department
- *change* his mind
- *change or implement* a procedure
- *increase* my bonus

There's a list of active verbs on the next page to help get you started thinking of active results:

ACTIVE VERBS

A

accelerate
adapt
address
administer
advise
analyze
apply
appoint
approve
arbitrate
arrange
assess
attain
audit
augment
author

B

bring
broaden
build

C

clarify
complete
conduct
consult
contact
coordinate
correct
create

D

develop
devise
diagnose
direct
discover
document

E

earn
edit
effect
eliminate
employ
enforce
engineer
establish
evaluate
examine
execute
exercise
expand
expedite
extract

F

facilitate
forecast
formulate
found

G

generate
guide

H

hesitate
hire

I

identify
improve
improvise
increase
influence
initiate
inspire
institute
instruct
insure

J

join
justify

K _____

kickstart

L _____

launch
lead
locate

M _____

measure
mediate
meet
mount

N _____

name
nominate
notify

O _____

obey
open
operate
order

P _____

paint
perform
pinpoint
pioneer
plan
prepare
present
print
procure
produce
program
project
propose
prove
provide
publish
purchase

Q _____

quadruple
qualify
quote

My Favorite Active Verbs Are: (List them here.)

New Active Verbs I'll Try to Use Soon: (List them here.)

R	S	U
recommend	schedule	undertake
reconcile	secure	unify
record	sell	
recruit	set up	
redesign	solve	**V**
reduce	sponsor	
regulate	staff	verify
reorganize	stimulate	
represent	strengthen	
research	structure	**W**
resolve	study	
restore	suggest	walk
review	supervise	wash
revise	survey	weave
		whittle
	T	**X**
	tailor	
	teach	Xerox
	test	
	train	
	translate	

MORE QUESTIONS TO ASK YOURSELF

Question 5: *Have I told my readers exactly what I want, at the beginning of my document?*

If you've found an active result, this part will be easy. One of the biggest favors I can do for my readers is to tell them what I'm talking about, right up front. Here are some examples: "I need your approval on hiring a Clown Troupe for the children's ward." " Can we meet to talk about my raise? " "We need to take action quickly or our computer system is going to crash."

CONCEPT #22:   *Get to the point–quickly.*

Making readers guess what I'm talking about until paragraph six is bad writing. If the readers know what my point is they'll be able to read what I have to say and absorb it more easily. If they don't know what the point is, they may never read what I've written at all. Or, they may read it after it's too late to do anything about the problem—then blame *me* for not alerting them. Worse yet, they may be frustrated each time they read anything I've written and aggravated every time they see a note from me.

Question 6:   *Have I stopped myself from telling everything to everyone?*

I make it a policy to tell readers *only* what *they need to hear*. If that means that they need only the big picture, I give them only the big picture. If they need lots of technical or procedural detail, I give them detail. If I'm writing to a mixed audience where some readers need only the big picture and others need lots of technical detail, I write a brief cover memo (or an executive summary) stating the big picture and attach a more detailed report for the people who need it. The surest way to bore readers is to tell the *whole* story.

CONCEPT #23:   *Don't tell the whole story.*

Write these concepts (three to five times each) on a separate page:

Concept #22	Concept #23	Concept #24
Get to the point quickly.	Don't tell the whole story.	Give them what *they* want in the order *they want it*.

Question 7: *Have I concentrated on being of service?*

In order to be really helpful to my readers, there are some things I have to take into consideration about readers in general:

- they're selfish
- they'll misunderstand whenever possible
- they're easily bored
- they've got a million things to read every day
- they're in a hurry

The questions I ask myself here are: "How can I help these harried, selfish readers (who are just like me) to understand what *they* need to know? " "How can I explain things in the simplest way? " "How can I write economically without wasting my time or trying my readers' patience? " One way to be sure you're on the right track is to be sure you've organized what you've written to make it easy for your readers to plow through it. We'll practice organizing in Chapter 5.

Please write your journal entry for Chapter 4 **NOW.** See Page 7 for instructions.

CHAPTER 5: GETTING ORGANIZED

Most people start organizing by chewing on the end of a pencil and looking up at the ceiling for inspiration. Then they scratch out a few things they want to say. Then they try to expand on those things. Usually this method leads to lackluster writing. It also promotes digression, and digressing is the last thing you want to be doing in your business communications. The method I'm going to suggest here has helped thousands of writers shave hours off their writing time. It creates a natural flow and leads you into a conversational voice that makes you think and write clearly. I discovered this method late in my career, but I count it as one of the most valuable things I've ever learned about writing.

FROM CHAOS TO ORGANIZATION EXERCISE

Stage One: Write your topic (what your document is about) in the space below. Keep it brief. Remember you're writing a topic, not a novel.

TOPIC

Stage Two: Write down who will be reading your document—by name if possible.

AUDIENCE(S)

Stage Three: Write the result you want—what you want the reader to *do* after he or she finishes reading your document. Use an active verb, e.g. sign, seal, deliver.

RESULT

IMPORTANT DIRECTIONS

Fold page 43 in half along the vertical line so that all you see is Column A.

Fill in column A.

Remember, the page is folded in half so you can only work with one column at a time.

Write everything *you want to **tell*** your audience (about your topic) in Column A.

Write your points down in any order they come into your head.

Don't try to write a formal outline. We'll talk about what you do in Column B later.

COLUMN A Things I (the writer) want to tell my readers	COLUMN B Questions I (the reader) have about this topic

When you've finished this column, turn immediately to the next page.

Now that you've completed Column A, I want you to change your perspective entirely. I want you to become the *reader*.

From this point on, I want you to see everything from the *reader's* point of view. And now, instead of listing the points you want *to tell* the reader, I want you to *ask the questions* your readers would have if all they saw was your topic. That's right. I want you to ask as many questions as you can from your *reader's* point of view.

Turn the page back so you can see *only* Column B. List all the questions that *the readers* would ask if they'd heard only the *topic* of your document. I'm going to say it again just to make sure you're clear about what I want you to do. **List all the questions that *the readers* would ask if they'd heard only the *topic* of your document.** If you don't remember your topic, turn back to the page on which you wrote it. Your topic may look like this: *PR Training Manual; North American Attitudes about French Canadians; Irish Outhouse Songs from the 1940s.* Whatever your topic is, this is all your reader knows about what you're writing. Naturally, this reader will have questions. Your job is to write those questions in Column B.

1.   Write the questions *in question form*, e.g. *How does this benefit me? How much is it going to cost? Why are you writing me about this? What would happen if we just ignored this until it started to cause big trouble?*

2.   List the questions that the readers *really* want answered. Try to hear the reader's voice. If the reader will be angry at what you're about to tell him, hear him yelling. If your reader wants every detail, hear her asking for every detail.

3.   Write your reader's questions in the order they come to you. Don't try to prioritize.

    Do it NOW.

Have I asked questions from my reader's point of view?

In order to know how to be a help to my readers I have to step out of *my own* shoes and into *theirs*. I need to imagine that I am *the reader* and all I know about the document in front of me is its *topic*: "Closing the San Francisco office," "Changes in the Summer Internship Program," "Giving me a huge raise."

Okay, as the *reader*, what questions do I ask myself immediately? Be *honest*. Here are some sample reader questions about the Summer Internship Program:

> *What's* in it for me?
> *Why* do we need to change the internship program?
> *Why* isn't the present internship system working?
> *How* does it benefit us to change it?
> *How* much will it cost?
> *Where* will we build it?
> *What* changes do we need to make?
> *Why* can't we just scrap the whole program?
> *When* do we need to do this?
> *Who's* going to be responsible for getting it done?
> *Is* there anyway to get another department to pay for this?
> *Is* there anyway to get another department to administrate this?
> *What* do I have to do about it?
> > approve the changes?
> > pass the suggestion on to my boss?
> > give the department money?
> > name a team to investigate the pros and cons?

How does writing from the reader's point of view affect your reader's interest in what you write? **Write your answer in the space below.**

Were there things in Column A that didn't show up in Column B?
Write them in the space below.

What did you discover after doing this exercise?
Write your discovery in the space below.

After you've listed all the things your readers *really* want to hear about, renumber them in the order of their importance *to the reader*. Like this.

1.   *most* important (to the reader)

10.   least important (to the reader)

Cut whatever is repetitive, insignificant or unrelated to the topic.

Write your newly ordered questions on a separate piece of paper.

Answer the questions in the order they now appear. Don't repeat them, don't use them as headings—just answer them as fully as you can. So, if the reader's question is: "Why do we need to reformulate the Poison Ivy Shampoo? " your answer should begin: "We need to reformulate the Poison Ivy Shampoo because…" If your reader's question is: "Isn't this going to cost a carload of money? " your answer should begin: "R & D has estimated the cost of reformulating the Poison Ivy Shampoo at $750,000, which is less than the lawsuits will cost us if all our customers come down with a nasty rash."

CUTTING AND PASTING

Looks good, doesn't it? You've come a long way since that first blank screen. Your draft is still messy, but most of what you need is there on paper and you're ready to cut and paste.

The first thing I look for in my draft is anything repetitious, or off the subject, or that doesn't move the story along. It's like liposuction—I'm in the position of the plastic surgeon, getting rid of the fat. The more extraneous stuff I remove, the clearer the document becomes.

MORE QUESTIONS TO ASK YOURSELF

Question 8:   *Have I rearranged the questions in the order that they are most important to my reader?*

This is the most important step because this is the step that will keep my readers reading. They'll keep reading because I've anticipated what *they* want to know, and I'm telling them in exactly the order *they* want to know it. Once you have your questions in the proper order, and you've answered them on a separate piece of paper, you have material that's custom-tailored to what your audience needs and wants to know. Material that's guaranteed to keep your readers reading—not because they *have* to, but because they *want* to.

CONCEPT #24:   *Give them what they want in the order they want it.*

Question 9:   *Have I moved the result I want (as a result of reading this document, my reader will...) as close to the top of the page as possible?*

Let's say the topic I'm writing about is *"budget approval"* for new machinery so that my firm, "Top Model Cosmetics" can produce a monobrow eyebrow thickener. What's the *result* I want from my reader in response to this request? Right. I want my reader to *approve* the budget I'm proposing. So, instead of starting this way:

"As you know, all our machinery is geared to the production of eyebrow thinners and tamers. Since we plan to introduce a monobrow eyebrow thickener this fall, we'll need $2,000,000 worth of new machinery."

I start by saying exactly what I want the reader to *do* for me, and or my department, like this:

"I'm writing to ask you to approve the new machinery budget for our eyebrow thickener production department..."

Two other openings for different requests that put the result I want right at the top of the document are:

"The research department will run out of Petri dishes in two weeks. Can you increase our standard order and rush delivery so we can continue our project without delay?"

"Thank you so much for suggesting I take this writing course. It's saved me weeks of time and trouble. I'd urge you to recommend it to other Research Analysts."

There are a couple of immediate benefits to putting the result you want at, or near, the beginning of your document: **first**, you're telling your reader exactly why you're writing. Now they don't have to work their way through three paragraphs of background material before they figure it out.

Second, you've stated exactly what you want, so you'll need to make everything else you write focus solely on getting your readers to do what you want them to do.

Here are some brief documents. The *results* the writers want are hidden in the body copy. Can you find those results? Don't *move* them. Just find them and mark them. You'll find Hidden Results Documents Example A on the next page.

HIDDEN RESULTS DOCUMENTS: EXAMPLE A

As you have seen in the last several weeks, each business unit within the company is re-affirming its strategic direction, business plan and budget. With that assessment comes the need to appropriately size the cost structure to support the level of revenue as well as look for opportunities to further re-engineer.

After in-depth analysis and review with business organizations, we realize the need to make some changes. I am sorry to say, in some instances, this will mean several of our colleagues will be leaving the company as we adjust the services we provide and our staff costs to be commensurate with the size of the businesses we service.

This also means we need to refocus our attention on supporting programs that drive revenue in growth as well as seek incremental cost reduction opportunities around the globe. Ongoing re-engineering and cost management programs will be a priority for our organization during fiscal year 2010.

Complete this sentence "In Example A, the writer wants the reader to...."

Write the completed sentence here:

HIDDEN RESULTS DOCUMENTS: EXAMPLE B

The New Jersey Casino Control Commission realized the need for a program to address compulsive gambling concerns years ago. In cooperation with the casino industry, community and state organizations, the Commission established the Self-Exclusion Program. The program allows people with a gambling problem to voluntarily exclude themselves from casino gaming activities in Atlantic City. The major area of enticement for compulsive gamblers is solicitation from the casino industry. Complimentary goods and services offered by a casino increased individuals' propensity to gamble in the facility. If you are a compulsive gambler and join the Self-Exclusion Program, you will not be able to receive complementary goods or services, credit or check cashing privileges.

Complete this sentence "In Example B, the writer wants the reader to...."

Write the completed sentence here:

HIDDEN RESULTS DOCUMENTS: EXAMPLE C

We are looking for talented people to work in our consulting company. Our purpose is to build a creative and professional environment in a company, to focus on future growth. As far as everybody understands, we work in the productive multi-talented environment: Technicians and Sales Representatives, Investors and Students, Customers, Clients and Vendors. We hope to attract new people to help us in developing and realizing our future plans.

We invite skilled professionals to a meeting, July 1 in Conference Room 38D at 111 Broadway. You are welcome to bring your résumé and new ideas. Be ready to analyze the situation on a market and discuss the advantages or disadvantages of computer products and possible projects.

We now have immediate opportunities for systems professionals to join our team. If your qualifications meet our needs, we would like to hear from you. We offer competitive salaries and benefit packages. Send résumés and salary requirements to: Hot Topic, International, 111 East 89th Street, New York, NY 10038.

Complete this sentence: "In Example C, the writer wants the reader to...."
Write the completed sentence here:

ANSWER KEY: HIDDEN RESULT DOCUMENTS

EXAMPLE A: *"The writer wants the reader to agree to cutting costs and revamp programs."*

EXAMPLE B: *"The writer wants the reader to sign up for the Self-Exclusion Program."*

EXAMPLE C: *"The writer wants the reader come to a meeting on July 1, to bring his/her résumé and be ready to discuss computer-products projects."*

Look at something you wrote for your office before you started this course. Find the place where you say what you want *your* readers to do when they finish reading. **Do it NOW.**

Was the result you wanted easy to find? Was it near the beginning of your document? If you've answered "yes" to both these questions, congratulations. Even if you haven't answered "yes" to the questions, take a few minutes to practice writing the results you want in the opening sentences for these situations:

a.	*Invitation*
b.	*Changed meeting time*
c.	*New technical procedure*
d.	*Cover letter for order for new equipment*
e.	*Request for outside supplier to give presentation at your offices*

Write your journal entry for Chapter 5 **NOW.** For instructions, see Page 7.

CHAPTER 6: USING HOOK AND LADDER TRANSITIONS

Transitions are the way to get a smooth flow of ideas from sentence to sentence and paragraph to paragraph. Transitions link ideas and identify the relationships between them. The Hook and Ladder Transition system works to avoid the standard transitions in favor of linking ideas *organically* within the paragraphs themselves.

From the time I learned how to write, people told me that I needed transitions to get from one paragraph to another. Nothing to argue with there. But then those same people handed me an extra-long list of "transition words." Words like: "therefore," "however" and "in conclusion." These words, and others like them, always appear on the standard transitions list. They *can* serve a purpose if you use them properly.

STANDARD TRANSITIONS LIST

		Transitions I Always Use:
for example	in spite of	(List them here.)
in particular	similarly	_____
nonetheless	on the other hand	_____
consequently	thus	_____
hence	yet	_____
for instance	still	_____
but	moreover	_____
furthermore	too	_____
also	besides	_____
in addition	now	_____
later	since that time	_____
first	next	_____
second	then	_____
third	finally	_____
that is	whereas	_____

I think the words on this list are bulky, empty, worthless words. They don't help me get from paragraph, to paragraph. They take up my time and they don't hold my interest. They do, however, serve a purpose. They smooth out rough edges and provide a rhythm for your facts and information.

TRANSITION EXERCISE #1

Unnecessary though I think these words are, let's see what would happen if we didn't use them. First read "Peter and Madonna" in the paragraph below *aloud*, *without* the transitions.

PETER AND MADONNA (WITHOUT TRANSITIONS)

"Peter and Madonna thought they loved each other very much. _____ they decided to move in together. _____ they opened a joint bank account. _____ Peter was married and had two children. _____ Peter had to get a divorce. _____ he had to find an apartment for his wife and kids. _____ he had to find enough money to pay for the new apartment he was sharing with Madonna.

_____ Madonna wasn't working and couldn't afford to pay for her half of the place. _____ Peter went to work as a bartender in a neighborhood bar.

_____ he hasn't seen his wife or his kids or Madonna.

_____ he met Amelie one night at the bar. _____ he moved with Amelie to France, far away from his wife and kids. _____ Peter and Amelie live happily in Provence."

How did it sound? Choose one or more: (a) fine (b) confusing (c) choppy

Turn to the previous page. Fill in the missing transitions. Read it aloud again.

How does it sound this time?

ANSWER KEY: PETER AND MADONNA *WITH* TRANSITIONS

"Peter and Madonna thought they loved each other very much. *So* they decided to move in together. *Later,* they opened a joint bank account. *But* Peter was married and had two children.

Hence, Peter had to get a divorce. *Then* he had to find an apartment for his wife and kids. *In addition,* he had to find enough money to pay for the new apartment he was sharing with Madonna.

But, Madonna wasn't working and couldn't afford to pay for her half of the place. *Consequently,* Peter went to work as a bartender in a neighborhood bar. *Since that time,* he hasn't seen his wife or his kids or Madonna.

On the other hand, he met Amelie one night at the bar. *Soon* he moved with Amelie to France, far away from his wife and kids. *Now* Peter and Amelie live happily in Provençe."

If you'd rather write a transitionless story, I recommend trying the Hook and Ladder Method. You'll find an explanation on the next page.

THE HOOK AND LADDER METHOD

The Hook and Ladder method works by repeating and reformulating key words or key ideas, and by using pronouns that refer to (or contain) the nouns used in previous sentences.

EXAMPLE

Sue-Ann's Case History

"Sue-Ann's fear that Roger would bite her thigh was, of course, the key factor in her inability to reach climax. However, not all non-climactic women focus on a *single* fear that's as specific and conscious as Sue-Ann's thigh-biting paranoia. Many women have *multiple* and *unconscious* fears that prevent them from reaching a climax."

Notice that Sue-Ann's case is stated in capsule form in the first sentence (followed by a "However,") and referred to again in the next sentence, in case the reader forgot what her problem was.

The *italics* in the second sentence *also* serve a transitional function, telling the reader that she will now see a *comparison* between single-focus conscious fears and multiple-focus unconscious ones.

There are other ways to get from one paragraph to another. One is to use a one-sentence summary of what you said in the preceding paragraph, followed by a sentence that starts with one of the transition words.

The thought pattern that leads you into the Hook and Ladder method is:

Tell- 'em-what-you're-gonna-tell-'em.

Tell-'em.

Tell-'em -what-you-told-'em.

Looking at key words again, let's imagine the paragraphs in a document as the rungs on a ladder. The rungs are spaced just widely enough apart so you can't reach from one rung to the next by using your hands. You *can* get to the next rung with a specially designed hook: 🪝 The trick for using the hook successfully is knowing exactly where to place it on each rung of the ladder. I'm going to **boldface** each hook the author uses so you can see where it falls in an actual document:

HOOK AND LADDER PICTURE OF ACTUAL DOCUMENT

"I'm stepping out of the usual format for this column because it's my last one. My term 🪝 **as president** is coming to an end.

The last **two years** 🪝 **as president** have been wonderful for me. When I was 🪝 **vice president,** the Board adopted a vision of becoming a dynamic presence in every community. During these 🪝 past two years, we have 🪝 **opened offices** in every state as well as the District of Columbia, the Virgin Islands and Puerto Rico.

I'm so proud that I was here to witness this 🪝 **fantastic achievement.**

It's been 🪝 **a great time for me** and for the company. And I'm sure it will be 🪝 **a great time for** Mark Denalovy Rosvadamsky, who becomes our **new** 🪝 **president on January 1.**"

Question: How do these hooks connect one paragraph to the next one? **Write your answer below:**

Here's another document where the Hook and Ladder method works nicely. Can you find the hooks? There are six of them.

HOOK AND LADDER PARAGRAPH #1

(Please cover the Answer Key before your begin.)

"Many employees feel that our program should be linked to annual salary increases.

They believe that salary increases would provide a much better incentive than current cash awards for exceptional service.

These employees believe that their supervisors consider the cash awards a satisfactory alternative to salary increases.

Although I don't think this practice is widespread, the fact that the employees believe that it is justifies a reevaluation of the merit awards program."

ANSWER KEY: HOOK AND LADDER PARAGRAPH #1

"Many employees feel that our program should be linked to annual 🪝**salary increases.**

They believe that 🪝**salary increases** would provide a much better incentive than current 🪝**cash awards** for exceptional service.

These employees believe that their supervisors considered the 🪝**cash awards** a satisfactory alternative to 🪝**salary increases**.

Although I don't think this practice is widespread, the fact that the employees believe that it is justifies a reevaluation of the merit 🪝**awards** program."

Try finding the hooks in the paragraph below. There are nine hooks. (Cover the answer key first.)

HOOK AND LADDER PARAGRAPH #2

"I need your approval on hiring temporary help in the left- handed wing-nut department. This temp would work only two days a week when the workload is heaviest.

Temporary help would cost only $80 a day with no benefits. Hiring a temp would save us two man-hours per day, per left-handed wing-nut employee.

Can you send me the approved forms by Tuesday so the new temp can start early next week? "

ANSWER KEY: HOOK AND LADDER PARAGRAPH #2

"I need your **approval** on **hiring temporary help** in the **left-handed wing nut** department. This **temp** would work only two days a week—when the workload is heaviest.

Temporary help would cost only $80 a day with no benefits.
Hiring a temp to would save us two man-hours per day, per **left-handed wing-nut** employee.

Can you send me your **approved** forms by Tuesday so the new **temp** can start early next week? "

WRITING A BIO EXERCISE

Biographies, the kind many of us write every time we change jobs, are great practice for using different kinds of transitions because biographies are both logical and sequential.

Try the exercise on the next page:

FAMOUS PERSON BIOGRAPHY
(an exercise in hook and ladder transitions)

Please read these suggestions and follow them carefully.

Choose a career, personality and persona from the list below.

Invent a name to go with the personality and career you've chosen.

Choose a city and state in the United States where your person grew up.

Choose a city and state where your person lives now.

FAMOUS PERSON CAREER CHOICES

famous film director	Nobel Prize-winning historian
successful stockbroker	presidential candidate
newspaper magnate	eminent archaeologist
world-famous plastic surgeon	world-famous architect
prominent opera star	professional stunt-man/woman
wealthy founder of a national toy store chain	distinguished philanthropist
distinguished psychologist	celebrated abstract artist
founder of successful chain of fast-food restaurants	universally-adored author of children's books

DIRECTIONS: Write a brief biography of the person you've chosen to be. Remember to use the *third person singular* in describing this person's life and accomplishments. Keep your bio brief—250 words is more than enough. Keep it fun, keep it interesting, keep it outrageous. Your goal is to make your reader want to meet the person whose bio it is.

Remember to isolate your **topic, audience** and **result (TAR)** and to list questions from your reader's point of view before you begin.

Write your bio on a separate sheet of paper. Do it **NOW**.

CLOSING WITH A "CALL TO ACTION"

By now, you've practiced trimming your document and you've put the result you want as close as possible to the beginning of the documents you write. That should be it, right? Well, *almost.* You have a clear straightforward opening, an interesting middle and (until now) no close.

Closes are easy if you have a strong "call to action." "Call to action" is really a nice way to say "demand," as in "Sit down!" "Come over here!" and "While you're up, bring me a Perrier."

The "call to action" is the last thing your readers read and the first thing they remember—so don't throw it away. Use it to repeat or reinforce what you want your reader to do as a result of reading your document. Here are some examples of call-to-action closes:

"Call me on Monday and we'll set up a meeting."

"Please tell Mice-R-Us to increase our standard order to 1,000 mouse ears and drop ship them to us ASAP."

"WMW-TV desperately needs your help now—and hopes you'll send us your contribution before sundown so we can continue broadcasting."

Let's say you've got a strong opening that says why you're writing, a nice way of getting from the opening sentence to the end—so now what? You have three choices:

1. *You can **summarize** what you've already said*

2. *You can **draw a conclusion** from what you've already said*

3. *Or, you can **tell** your readers **what** you want them **to do next***

I find, in business writing, my most effective close is the one where I tell the readers exactly what I want them to do. I call this close a "call to action." Look over some of your recent office correspondence. Find five of your weakest closes. Write them on a separate page, exactly as they appeared in your documents. Then change them into call to action closes. **Do it NOW.**

Take a few moments now to practice writing strong calls to action. Write a call to action for each of the following issues. You don't have to write the entire document—just write the call to action for:

a. *Overdue check*
b. *Dear John letter (This is the letter you write to break up with someone, e.g., "Dear John I'm marrying Harry. Goodbye.")*
c. *Note to dry cleaner who ruined your shirt*
d. *Request for someone's time*
e. *Request for information*
f. *Love letter*
g. *Request for large donation*

Please write your journal entry for Chapter 6 **NOW.** For instructions, see Page 7.

CHAPTER 7: ORGANIZING INTERNATIONAL COMMUNICATION

Once you know *what* you're talking about and *to whom* you're talking, you'll want to organize what you want to say. Writing styles differ from culture to culture and from person to person. The more business I do with an international audience, the more important it is for me to understand as much as I can about my reader and my reader's cultural style. I also need to be careful to avoid all idioms (clauses or phrases that are significant in our culture, but meaningless elsewhere). "He bought the farm" may mean "he died" in Newark, but it's just an untranslatable message in Minsk. Phrasal verbs (a verb + a preposition) which we use all the time are confusing to others because they don't have anything to do with literal meanings. What would you do if you had to translate *break up, push around,* or *sound off* into Mandarin? You see the problem.

Each culture has its own ideas about organization, too. Once you're aware of what's going on, you can imitate the style and get your message across more effectively.

ASIAN STYLE (for example) circles around with elaborate greetings and questions about health and family and wishes for success until it finally arrives at the point.

✖ = the point

Example: "Forgive me for not writing you for such a long time. It was before winter when I wrote you last. It's spring now. I like this season very much. I hope it is getting warmer in New York, too. The family's well and I wonder if you could lend me $147,000? "

LATIN STYLE starts out on its way to the point but finds itself throwing in extra information about vacations, activities, gifts and other things that have nothing to do with the point. The message keeps on moving *toward* the point and it gets there eventually.

Example: "I've been working with Bunny Sanhedran to get figures for the fourth quarter. Bunny's just returned from her honeymoon in Mexico where she and her husband spent two months pressing tortillas, so it will take another week or so 'til she finds everything she needs for the estimates. She brought jalapeno jelly home for everyone in the department and I'll bring you a jar when I deliver the fourth quarter numbers sometime next Friday."

RUSSIAN STYLE begins with lots of very dramatic extraneous detail then hits you suddenly with the raw, unvarnished point.

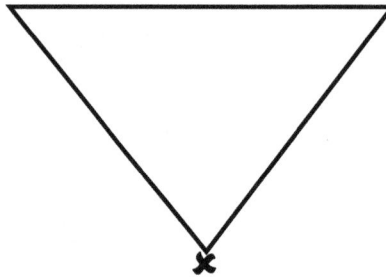

Example: "There was this tremendous accident. Fifty-seventh Street was tied up for three blocks. A car hit a bus and dozens of people were being carried off to ambulances. I've never seen anything like it. And that's why I'm late."

AMERICAN STYLE looks like a baseball diamond. It starts right out with the point, expands on it, and then repeats the point at the end.

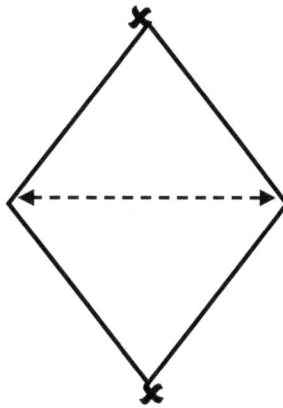

Example: "Southern California is a marvelous place to visit because of its pleasant weather and its beautiful natural habitats: (*the author makes his point*) mountains, ocean, deserts, forests and a constant temperature of 72 sunny, beautiful degrees make every trip a delight. (*the author expands on his point with examples*) … So California is well worth visiting because of its wonderful weather and its wide variety of natural settings." (*the author wraps it up by reinforcing his point*)

Each style talks directly to its readers and fulfills its readers' expectations. If you mix cultural styles, sending an Asian-style memo to American-style readers, the Asian-style memo frustrates the American readers because American readers are used to information that *gets right to the point*.

Sending an American-style letter to an Asian reader convinces the Asian reader that Americans are rude because they lack the formulaic niceties Asian readers expect. Knowing what style of communication your reader is used to is crucial if you want to get your point across without ruffling feathers.

A Russian friend of mine, who works at a large consulting firm, operates in an international environment. She sends American organizational-style e-mail to her team in New York and Asian-style e-mail to her clients in Tokyo. This cultural sensitivity has polished her style-change skills so she can switch from Asian to

American-style quickly and easily—and still write Russian-style letters to her family in Moscow.

In this book, we'll be talking exclusively about the American-style communication and the different task-specific ways to approach organizing material in the American style.

CONCEPT #25:   Put the result you want first.

The quickest, easiest way to organize material that runs two or three pages (or less) is to look over your list of reader's questions and objections. Since you've already organized these in the order to which they are most *important to your reader*, you've created an instant plan for your finished document. Now all you have to do is **start with the result** (what you want your readers to *do*), answer the questions *in the order you've listed them* (you've already done this part). Then add a strong "call to action."

Remember: a "call to action" tells readers exactly what you want from them, for example: "Please call Donna as soon as you can, then let me know by Thursday, June 8, exactly what problems she has with the DooHickey Program." or " I'll call you next Monday to see if we can find a time to meet in person."

An effective American-style business writing pattern looks like this:

Beginning	result statement + consumer benefit*
Middle	readers' questions answered in order of importance to them
End	call to action

*A *consumer benefit* is the answer to the readers' question, *"What's in it for me?"*

,

DISCOVERY EXERCISE   DO THIS EXERCISE NOW.

Take a look at the last (page-long) letter or memo you wrote. Did you follow an effective business writing pattern? If not, what does your pattern look like?

Many people's writing patterns look like this:

Beginning	**background of the situation or problem (sometimes going back as far as the ice age)**
Middle	**consequences of the problem or situation.**
End	**actions that need to be taken, plus "if you have any questions, please call me."**

The problem with organizing your correspondence this way is that your readers have to read through to the end of the middle section to figure out what you want them to do, or even why they're on your mailing list. So much for beginnings and middles.

I have a pet peeve about endings, especially the ending, "If you have any questions, please call me." I'm going to tell you about the peeve and I'm going to explain why any correspondence that ends "If you have any questions, please call me" makes me hopping mad. Anyone who's foolhardy enough to end an e-mail to me with this line gets this return message: "Yes, I have three questions—'What is the meaning of life? ' 'What do men really want? ' and 'Why do my eyebrows grow back faster than my fingernails? ' Please get back to me by Thursday with the answers."

Let's assume you're communicating with adults. *All* adults know that if they have questions, they can call or e-mail you. While you may believe that inviting questions is polite or leaves an opening, telling them to call you insults their intelligence and wastes their time. Besides, it's become such a standard closing nobody even reads it. If you really want your readers to call you, put your phone number under the typed version of your name at the end of the letter or e-mail, so your readers can find it easily.

CONCEPT #26:   *Last read, first remembered.*

Here's another reason I don't like the "if you have any questions…" ending: the end of anything you write is the most *powerful* part of your document. It calls your readers to action, or makes an unforgettable statement. Imagine if American Patriot Patrick Henry instead of saying "Give me liberty, or give me death!" had said "Give me liberty or give me death and if you have any questions please call me." See if removing "If you have any questions, please call me," doesn't strengthen what you've written. See if anyone calls you to complain.

CONCEPT #27:   *Use the right style for the right purpose.*

This is advanced work; one style may not work for everything. You wear one type of clothes to go sailing and another to a wedding. You'd never wear the sailing clothes to a formal event. Nor would you wear a tuxedo or evening gown for a day sail. Similarly, you need to have a wardrobe of organizational styles to handle specific correspondence situations. You wouldn't start a condolence note with what you want the reader to do as soon as he/she finishes reading, for example. (*Dear Gertrude, Please call me if there's anything I can do for you…*) But you <u>would</u> start the answer to a complaint with an apology. (*Dear Mr. Hammerhead, We're very sorry to hear about the trouble you've been having with your Icelandic Track and hope you'll be out of traction and on the mend soon.*)

Write these concepts (three to five times each) on a separate page:

Concept #25	Concept #26	Concept #27
Put the result I want *first.*	Last read, first remembered.	Use the right style for the right purpose.

AMERICAN ORGANIZATIONAL STYLES

Here are nine different organizational styles that will come in handy for most projects you'll face on the job:

REQUEST

Beginning   Say what you need or want:

"I need your signature on this...."

Middle   Explain why you want it:

"...so we can move forward with the HairCurler project...."

End   Express your gratitude for any help that might be forthcoming:

"I'd be very grateful if I could have the signed original contract back on my desk by Monday, October 21. Thanks for your help"

Notice I did not say: "Thanking you in advance for your attention to this matter." I didn't say it because (1) thanking people for something you're pressuring them to do is rude (2) it's such a worn-out old phrase (3) it sounds bureaucratic and stuffy. A comedy writer once said that the only time it's appropriate to write "thanking you in advance," is in a ransom note.

REQUEST FOR INFORMATION OR APPROVAL

Beginning   Say why you're writing:

"We've run into a snag on the mouse-ear lab tests...."

Middle	List what you need and why: *"We need 200 more short-tailed white mice immediately to complete the trials."*
End	Call for reader to take specific action: *"Can you requisition the mice from Medical Supply and have them delivered to the J. Edgar Hoover Lab before the end of November?"*

"ATTABOY"/"ATTAGIRL"

(LETTER COMMENDING A JOB WELL-DONE)

Beginning	State what you're writing for, e.g. to commend, to thank: *"Your tech people, Colin and Patrick, made my job so easy last week. Thank you for assigning them to my seminar."*
Middle	Describe the situation. Include personal details: *"They got to the conference room early and helped me set up.* *They were there for me when I ran into trouble.* *They calmed me down when I got my belt caught in my USB cable."*
End	Repeat your gratitude and say what the experience did for you: *"I'm so grateful to have had them I'd like to pack them in my 'emergency seminar kit' and take them everywhere I go."*

PERSONAL THANK-YOU NOTE

Beginning   Describe exactly what you're thanking them for:

"Dear Aunt Dottie, Your handsome hand-knit 'Tower of London' tea cozy arrived this morning."

Middle   Tell how you feel about it:

"Jim and I have never seen anything quite like it. We cherish it and every time we have tea, we think of you."

End   Thank sender for the thought:

"Thank you so much for thinking of us."

BUSINESS THANK-YOU NOTE

Beginning   Describe what you're thanking them for:

"Thank you for the multi-million-dollar tour of the West Street Seaport..."

Middle   Tell them how you feel:

"I can't remember when I've learned so much in so short a time. It was fascinating to see West Street from an insider's point of view..."

End   Express desire to repeat the activity:

"Let's have lunch again soon. Meanwhile, I'll think of ways I can help you with your promotion plans."

CONDOLENCE

Beginning   Express your feelings on hearing the news:

"I was so sorry to hear about Christine."

Middle   Describe your thoughts about, or personal relationship with, the deceased and what it meant to you:

"She gave me my first job in publishing, and we've been friends ever since. She was warm and funny and as generous as all outdoors. I'll miss her greatly."

End   Offer condolences/Offer help:

"Please accept my condolences, and prayers. I'll call you next week to see if there's anything I can do to help you through this difficult time."

SALES

Beginning   Get the readers' attention with an interesting or shocking opening:

"If you lost your job today, and all the money you had to live on for the rest of your life was in your savings account, how long would the money last?"

Middle   Describe the consumer benefits of the product or service. Include as much detail as is appropriate:

"You probably don't have to worry about this because you have an Estate Plan that you've been building for decades. Nor do you worry about long-term care because you've already made plans for it." *

* This is a backwards way of posing a consumer benefit. It creates a shiver of fear in the reader and makes considering the benefits of Estate planning seem surprisingly attractive.

End	Create a sense of urgency or strong call to action

"If you are worried, you need to move as quickly as possible. Each day you delay may wipe out your bank account and leave your family desperate. I'll be happy to give you all the details. Just put your name and address on the RSVP card and send it back to me so I can begin a personal profile for you."

COLLECTION

Beginning	Politely suggest that payment may have been overlooked. Give details of what's due:

"You may have overlooked our March invoice ($657.35) for eight cases of Lavender's Liquid Brilliantine."

Middle	Ask for the money:

"We've enclosed a self-addressed envelope for your check, so you won't have to wait for the next billing cycle.

End	State the consequences for non-compliance:

"If we haven't received your check by February 2, we'll add a 25% late fee to your next bill."

COMPLAINT

Beginning   State exactly why you're complaining. Describe the situation you're complaining about:

"I'm writing to say that the Giorgio Armani dress-shirt you laundered was returned to me—ruined. There was lipstick and powder on the collar. There were three missing front buttons. The cuffs were frayed, and there was a tear above the right elbow."

Middle   Explain the effect the situation has had on you:

"As a direct result of the condition the shirt was returned in, my wife believes I'm having a tempestuous affair. She's left me and taken the dog."

End   State exactly what you want:

"I would like Madame LaFarge Cleaners to reimburse me for my loss, send me a check for $400.00, and see if they can recover my dog."

REJECTION

Beginning   Express regrets that you cannot use/buy/contribute to (or whatever your correspondent has written you about) at this time:

"I'm sorry to say that Toxic Chemical Waste Industries cannot use your photographs."

Middle   Say you'll be in touch if the situation changes:

"If the situation changes, someone from this office will be in touch with you."

End   Send thanks and well-wishes:

"Thanks for your interest in Toxic Chemical Waste Industries, and best of luck with your project."

The Beginning/Middle/End methods work fine for one or two page documents, but say you've got a lengthy report due at the end of the week? How do you organize *that*?

ORGANIZING REPORTS

CHRONOLOGICAL: The "Who, What, When, Where and Why? " Method

Your bank is moving from the East Side to the West Side and merging with Goldfinger, Staks, Meagher and Flim-Flam Securities. You need to tell Purchasing about the move so that all employees have new stationery and business cards ready when they arrive at the new building.

- ◆   List the sequence of events in the order they will happen
- ◆   Say which departments or people will be affected
- ◆   Give dates if possible

Mailroom Stationery Schedule for Merger

Date	January 13	January 26	February 2	February 5	March 5
Task	Collect stationery orders from each department.	Place order with printer.	Receive new stationery. Check for errors.	Mail stationery to all branches.	Collect all complaints. Send corrections to printer.
Person Responsible	Harold	Marcella	Roger	Justin	Tiffany

PROCEDURAL: The "First You Plug It In..." Method

You're going on maternity leave. You need to tell your department head, and whoever fills in for you, how to do your job.

Describe the procedure in successive steps:

1. come into office
2. make coffee
3. chat on phone with friends
4. check personal e-mail
5. go to lunch

GEOGRAPHIC: The Cartographer Method

All your customers at Wiley Widgets are moving from Atlanta to Seattle, Miami and Maine.

♦ State the issue
♦ Describe the effect on Wiley Widgets area by area
♦ Suggest how the company can deal with (or profit from) the situation

"Our customer base is shifting from Atlanta. We can no longer get widgets to them overnight, so longtime customers are switching to local suppliers. Opening northeast, southeast, and northwest service centers would solve our delivery problems and we could market our widgets to new local customers. Here are some avenues I think we should explore:"

CAUSE TO EFFECT: The "First This Happened-Then That Happened" Method

Your general contractor used Oopsee architectural supports in constructing the Pizza national headquarters building. Unfortunately, the Oopsee supports were unstable, so the Pizza building now leans left at a 45-degree angle.

State the issue.

"The instability of the Oopsee supports used to stabilize the Pizza building has caused problems throughout the company."

Describe the problems resulting from using wrong supports.

- *The building can no longer withstand crosswinds of more than two miles an hour*
- *It is in danger of falling over during hurricane season*
- *Employee health and safety have been seriously compromised*
- *The Pizza building has become an architectural laughingstock and is so listed in all the travel guides.*

EFFECT TO CAUSE: The "This Happened Because This and That Happened First" Method

You work for Bad Taste Novelties. All your Army Joe dolls were shipped wearing Darby doll ball gowns instead of regulation Army camouflage, and 99 % of the Army Joes were returned with irate letters.

State the effect the returns have had on BadTaste Novelties.

Then, explain what happened to lead to that effect.

"The return of 99 % of the Army Joe dolls shipped in ball gowns has caused a significant loss of business, a diminution of BadTaste stock value and a 70 % drop in sales during the third quarter.

"We've looked into what caused the dolls to go out inappropriately dressed. These are our findings:

1. *The factory in Taiwan was late in filling our camouflage uniform order*

2. *The mailroom chose to use an inexpensive shipping company (in compliance with our new frugality guidelines)*

3. *The carrier failed to deliver the uniforms to our shipping department in time to get orders to our accounts*

4. *The sales department decided it was better to send Army Joes out in ball gowns (which we had on hand) than to miss our ship date*

COMPARE AND CONTRAST: The "Mine is Bigger than Yours" Method

Your company, Worst Foods, is considering the acquisition of a business that makes anchovy-flavored ice cream.

Assess the current ice cream market.

Then, list the pros and cons of adding the new company's anchovy-flavored product to Worst Foods' current flavor mix.

- Marketing Research Inc. (MRI) reports that 99 % of companies in the ice cream market make sweet-tasting ice cream exclusively
- Their reports indicate a 58 % rise in sales of savory foods (e.g. pretzels and potato chips) in the last decade (2005-2015)
- There is no ice cream currently on the market designed to satisfy this taste for savory foods

Here is a list of pros and cons regarding Worst Foods introducing a new line of ice cream savories:

Con	Pro
♠ *consumer resistance to new idea*	✓ *consumer curiosity and taste for savories*
♠ *need for new suppliers*	✓ *open market niche*
♠ *packaging compatibility*	✓ *existing machinery okay*
	✓ *cost: savory ice cream cheaper than sweets*

CONCEPT #28:   *Bullets and numbers make points easier for readers to find.*

Write these concepts (three to five times each) on a separate page:

Concept #28	Concept #29	Concept #30
Bullets and numbers make points easier for readers to find.	Get to the point.	Use everyday words.

Please write your journal entry for Chapter 7 **NOW.** For instructions, see Page 7.

YOUR NOTES HERE

CHAPTER 8: AVOIDING EXCESS BLAH-BLAH

~~One of the things that annoys people most and causes them to throw your documents directly into the wastebasket,~~ People hate ~~is~~ wordiness, empty words, meaningless words, words most people use all the time but don't know why.

My friend Stefan calls this writing style, "excess blah-blah." The minute readers hit a patch of excess blah-blah, they leave. It's impossible to get them back.

In Chapter 8 we'll practice two sure-fire techniques for making wordy writing concise.

> "A sentence should contain no unnecessary words,
> a paragraph no unnecessary sentences, for the same
> reason that a drawing should have no unnecessary
> lines and a machine no unnecessary parts."
>
> The Elements of Style
> by W. Strunk and E. B. White
> (New York, Macmillan Co., 1959)

Whenever you help people get through your document quickly, you save them (very expensive) time. All that saved time is like money in the bank and will eventually find its way into *your* bank account.

~~Every time you~~ Cut out ~~an~~ unnecessary words and it's ~~like putting~~ money in the bank. ~~Why? Because~~ (T)he more quickly your readers read, the more they remember. Every extra word ~~you leave in what you write~~ slows your reader down.

One of the most effective ways of copyediting is to go on a "small word" hunt. This may surprise you, but there are 25 "small" words in the English language that take up 33% of our writing and speech. If you cut these words and rearrange your sentences, your writing will improve dramatically. You'll find the evil small word list on the next page.

EVIL SMALL WORD LIST

a	the	in	on	of
I	to	me	my	it
with	have	has	had	and
he	she	but	for	that
at	is	are	was	were

Small word hunting is an art that takes practice. Can you find all the small words in the following paragraphs? (Cover the Answer Key first).

SMALL WORD HUNTING EXERCISE #1: FIND 23

It is a matter of the gravest possible importance to the health of any man or woman with a history of a problem with disease of the heart that he or she should avoid the sort of foods with a high percentage of fats.

ANSWER KEY: SMALL WORD HUNTING EXERCISE #1

It is a matter of the gravest possible importance to the health of any man or woman with a history of a problem with disease of the heart that he or she should avoid the sort of foods with a high percentage of fats.

CAN YOU CONVEY THE IDEA OF THE SENTENCE ABOVE IN TEN WORDS?

Anyone with a history of heart disease should avoid fatty foods.

SMALL WORD HUNTING EXERCISE #2: FIND 24

HANDSTAND INCORPORATED

MEMO

From: Research Team   To: Management

    The Handstand research area in Moosejaw, Canada has become unbearable for the team. I have had numerous complaints including health issues; seating arrangements; pilferage; morale; air quality; lighting and cleanliness.

    The office manager does not seem to understand. I have made several complaints and it seems as if they have fallen on deaf ears. On many occasions, she said that she would try and come up with new arrangements, but those promises were never fulfilled.

ANSWER KEY: SMALL WORD HUNTING EXERCISE #2

HANDSTAND INCORPORATED

MEMO

From: Roger Dodger   To: Dolores Puppybreath
      Manager, Research Team   Vice President, Operations

    The Handstand research area in Moosejaw, Canada has become unbearable for the team. I have had numerous complaints including: health issues; seating arrangements; pilferage; morale issues; air quality; lighting and cleanliness.

    The office manager does not seem to understand. I have made several complaints and it seems as if they have fallen on deaf ears. On many occasions, she said that she would try and come up with new arrangements, but those promises were never fulfilled.

Please rephrase and rewrite Small Word Hunting Exercise #2. Use your own words. Your goal is to eliminate as many small words as possible. Remember to put your result first and to end with a call to action. Use a separate piece of paper. **Do it NOW.**

SUGGESTED ANSWER KEY:

REWRITE SMALL WORD HUNTING EXERCISE #2

(Your rewrite will probably differ from this one.)

HANDSTAND INCORPORATED

MEMO

From: Roger Dodger   *To: Dolores Puppybreath*
      Manager, Research Team   *Vice President, Operations*

Dolores, we need your help. I hear constant complaints about conditions in Moosejaw's research area including:

> *health issues*
> *seating arrangements*
> *pilferage*
> *morale issues*
> *air quality*
> *lighting*

I spoke with our office manager several times, yet our research area's condition remains unbearable.

Can you help us solve this problem? I'll call you Tuesday to see if there's anything we can do.

Look at any office correspondence you wrote *before* working with this book. Cut the small words and rearrange the piece. Compare your "before" and "after" version. **Do it NOW.**

84

Good writing doesn't waste words. A sentence may be long and detailed, but it shouldn't be redundant. In business writing, aim for brief, direct sentences and use easy- to-understand words.

CONCEPT #29:   *Get to the point.*

Edward T. Thompson, in an essay called "How to Write Clearly," published by International Paper Company, says:

> *Don't say:* The biota exhibited a 100% mortality response,
> *when you can say:* **all the fish died**.

CONCEPT #30:   *Use everyday words.*

Consider this paragraph:

"A number of indicators suggest that the bordello business is heating up. November sales this year were 57 % above the figures for November last year. But strong activity signs do not support an overheating scenario yet. Demand appears to have increased towards year-end, but supply also remains high."

Can you find the five empty phrases in the paragraph above?

CONCEPT #31: *Cut the fluff.*

> *"A number of"* is dead weight; so is *"yet."*

> *"Appears to have been"* is a wordy way of saying *"demand increased"*.

> *"Also"* doesn't add to the meaning of the sentence.

A good time to nuke excess blah-blah is when you copy edit. Look at what you've written, then delete any unnecessary words.

FIX WORDY SENTENCES

(1) Underline the most important words in the wordy sentence; and

(2) Make a sentence out of those words; use a *minimum* of linking words, then

(3) Play around with the word order until you have the *leanest* sentence possible

For example:

A. Underline the most important words in the sentence:

A number of indicators suggest that the <u>bordello business</u> is <u>heating up</u>. <u>Sales</u> in <u>November this year</u> (2044) were <u>57% above November last year</u>. But strong <u>activity</u> signs do <u>not support</u> an <u>overheating</u> scenario yet. <u>Demand</u> appears to have <u>increased</u> towards <u>year-end</u> but <u>supply</u> also remains <u>high</u>.

B. Make a sentence out of the underlined words only. Use a minimum of linking words. Make your sentence sound like a telegram.

bordello business… heating up… Sales… November 2044 …57% above November 2043 …activity…not support …overheating …demand increased… year-end… supply… high.

C. The Bordello business is heating up, but not *over*heating. November 2044 sales are 57% above November 2043 sales. Despite increased year-end demand, supply remains high.

CONCEPT #32: *Cut "empty words."*

Write these concepts (three to five times each) on a separate page:

Concept #31	Concept #32	Concept #33
Cut the fluff.	Cut empty words.	The more quickly I read the more I remember.

Trying to untangle convoluted sentences slows readers down. Instead of letting their eyes skim over a difficult sentence, readers stop, go back and try to unravel the sentence's meaning from the beginning. This stop-and-start action hampers reading speed, causes readers to forget what they read and makes it more difficult to connect with what they're about to read in the immediate future.

CONCEPT #33: *The more quickly you read, the more you remember.*

See how quickly you can read the following sentence and how accurately you can write down what it means. **Do it NOW.**

"Other unknowns that might hurt EDM in February, even if the broader global outlook remains favorable, include (1) the possibility of Russia going into technical default with the Paris Club; (2) a return of Turkish jitters, as the government continues its commendable efforts to keep its IMF program on track."

How'd you do? How many times did you have to reread the sentence to figure it out? How did rereading affect your ability to remember what was going on? The point is to keep it simple. Free your sentences from unnecessary convolution—keep your words concrete and memorable.

Write these concepts (three to five times each) on a separate page:

Concept #34	Concept #35	Concept #36
Prefer short words to long ones.	Put some life into it.	Check who's doing what in every sentence.

Let's go back to our first example:

Don't say: The biota exhibited a 100% mortality response,
when you can say: **all the fish died**.

Which one did you read quickly? Which one can you remember easily? Why? My guess is that you read **all the fish died** quickly because the words created an instant picture in your mind. The more pictures you create, the easier your writing is to read. "First Degree" words create concrete mental pictures instantly. If I say: "I was attacked by an animal in the forest," — my reader may see anything from a buffalo to a wild boar. That's because "animal" is a "Second Degree" word: a word that doesn't create a specific picture. If I say, "I was attacked by a gerbil," my reader will know exactly what went on in the forest.

SECOND DEGREE WORDS	VS.	FIRST DEGREE WORDS
ocean	Pacific
volume	book
visage	face
project	widget revamp

CONCEPT #34: *Prefer short words to long ones.*

Write these concepts (three to five times each) on a separate page:

Concept #37	Concept #38	Concept #39
Short sentences are easier to remember than long ones.	Cut the warm-up.	Verbs are stronger than nouns.

There are several mechanical ways to encourage your reader to read quickly. We'll look at some of them now.

CONCEPT #35:   *Put some life into it*

GET ACTIVE

Change from passive voice to active voice to clarify your sentences. If the main idea is to keep readers reading quickly, the passive voice stops readers cold. The passive voice makes readers go back to the beginning of the sentence or paragraph in a futile attempt to figure out what the writer means.

There are three problems with the passive voice:

1.   It's lengthy
2.   It's lifeless
3.   It's hard to remember

It's also difficult to figure out who is doing (or who did) what in a passive sentence. What *is* the passive voice? Keep reading, I'll tell you in a minute.

The simple, *active* voice English sentence pattern looks like this: Subject (the person or thing doing the action). Verb (the action). Object (the person or thing receiving the action). The pattern is "Who did it? What did he do? To whom did he do it? "

S   V   O

Active Voice Example: *My **pit bull** bit the **head mistress** at Brearly.*

The passive voice sentence pattern starts with the Object (the person receiving the action) is followed by some form of the Verb "to be"; then the Subject, if there is one.

Object   Verb (to be)   Subject

O   V   S

Passive Voice Example: *The **head mistress** at Brearly was bitten by **Jake**, my pit bull.*

CONCEPT #36:   *Check who's doing what in every sentence.*

I don't mean we should *never* use the passive voice. Writing in the passive voice is not a felony crime. When then-Vice President Al Gore was accused of using a White House telephone to make fund-raising calls, the press asked then-President Bill Clinton about the incident. Clinton's response was: "Mistakes were made." Passive voice. Apparently, nobody was making those mistakes. Clinton used the passive voice correctly to protect the Vice President.

There are times and places to use the passive voice. I'm not against the passive voice. I'm just against *over*using it.

Can you rewrite sentences A through D using the active voice? Remember to put people first. **Do it NOW.**

> A.   The lily was gilded by Daphne
>
> B.   The treasure was discovered up the creek by the pirate with the paddle
>
> C.   Mistakes were made
>
> D.   It was decided to give the writers a big bonus

Doesn't the rewrite sound better?

USE ONLY THE WORDS THAT GET YOUR MESSAGE ACROSS:

Redundant example: *Her dress was puce in color.*

Concise example: *Her dress was puce.*

Did you really need "in color?" Puce *is* a color; why say "color" twice?

CONCEPT #37: *Short sentences are easier to remember than long ones*

Maid Marianne's surrender is caused by *three related incidents.* ~~that happen throughout the play.~~

This novel will *clarify~~, explain, and make clear~~* the reasons for the new Second Avenue Subway.

He spent several *summer(s) ~~segments of his life~~* waiting tables at the Wharf by the Madison Beach Hotel.

AVOID STARTING SENTENCES WITH:

"There is," "There are," or "There were."

CONCEPT #38: *Cut the warm-up.*

~~There are~~ two things ~~which~~ come up in every meeting: tardiness and sloth.

~~There are~~ many goldfish ~~who~~ want to grow up to be sharks.

~~There were~~ *(The crew made)* 17 attempts to mutiny on the Bounty.

Occasionally, *there is, there are, or there were* can be used with good effect to open a paragraph ("There are two reasons for acting up.") or to line up the sentences in a list-structure paragraph ("There are fourteen ways to deal with this challenge."). Use these clauses with caution. Overuse leads to the "too much salt in the soup" effect. *Blechhh.*

WHEREVER POSSIBLE, GET RID OF ADJECTIVE CLAUSES LIKE:

"Who Are," "Which Was," and "That Had Been."

Vampires ~~who are~~ living in New Orleans have to feed four times a week.

The Puppybreath children bought a yacht, ~~which was~~ made entirely of prairie pine.

For many years the country was ruled by a ~~man who had been appointed by himself~~ *self-appointed* ~~as~~ dictator ~~of the country~~.

USE VERBS INSTEAD OF NOUNS AND NOUN PHRASES

CONCEPT #39: *Verbs are stronger than nouns.*

    A. The *donations* of the *alumni* to the sperm bank will be in *accordance* with their *understanding* of its *goals.* (noun phrases)

    B. Alumni *will donate* to the sperm bank if they *understand* its goals. (verbs)

    C. The motive for his decision to kill Martha was his quest to acquire her money. (noun phrases)

    D. He *killed* Martha because he *wanted* her inheritance. (verbs)

CONCEPT #40:   *Murder your darlings.*

We've talked about several methods of trimming your writing. But, if I can give you one tip that has done wonders for me, it's this: if you find a sentence or paragraph that you think is particularly witty or pithy or well-said—you **must** cut it out.

This is what professional writers refer to as *"murder your darlings."* The reason behind cutting those well-turned phrases, sentences and paragraphs is—they *always,* repeat, *always* dilute your primary message. Try removing your favorite things from the next memo you write at work and see if it isn't more to the point.

Caution: Cutting words can completely alter the *meaning* of your document. Read the Braintwisters below to see what I mean, then thoroughly check what you've edited to make sure it still says what you want it to say.

BRAINTWISTERS: A devilish collection of tongue-teasing story-puzzles

DIRECTIONS:

Goal: To reduce each Braintwister sentence to *one* word followed by an exclamation point.

Number of Players: One or more

In any one turn, you may take out one, two or three consecutive words.

You may change punctuation and/or capitalization.

You may *not* add words, rearrange words or change any endings.

(As you reduce the sentence the meaning changes, taking you to places you never thought you'd go.)

Each deletion must leave a grammatically correct sentence.

Read the sentence aloud after each turn to make sure it's grammatically correct and meaningful.

Here's an example:

Tourists in Athens

When Theo and Theda arrived in Athens on Thursday the 13th, they saw thousands of thieves running through the theater district with thick leather clothes.

Turn #1   (When) Theo and Theda arrived in Athens on Thursday the 13th, they saw thousands of thieves running through the theater district with thick leather clothes.

Turn #2   Theo and Theda arrived (in Athens) on Thursday the 13th; they sa w thousands of thieves running through the theater district with thick leather clothes.

Turn #3   Theo and Theda arrived on Thursday the 13th; they saw thousands of thieves running through the theater district with (thick) leather clothes.

Turn #4   Theo and Theda arrived on Thursday the 13th; they sa w thousands of thieves running through the theater district (with leather clothes).

Turn #5   Theo and Theda arrived on Thursday; (the 13th), they saw thousands of thieves running through the theater district.

Turn #6   Theo and Theda arrived on Thursday; they saw thousands of thieves running through the theater (district).

Turn #7   Theo and Theda arrived on Thursday; they saw thousands of thieves running (through the theater).

Turn #8   Theo and Theda arrived on Thursday; they saw (thousands of) thieves running.

Turn #9   Theo and Theda arrived on Thursday; they saw thieves(running).

Turn #10   Theo and Theda arrived (on Thursday); they saw thieves.

Turn #11   Theo and Theda (arrived; they) saw thieves.

Turn #12   (Theo and) Theda saw thieves.

Turn #13   Theda saw (thieves).

Turn #14   Theda (saw)!

Turn #15   Theda!

Here are two more Braintwisters. See what you can do with them:

Ruth's Tooth

"Forsooth!" said Ruth, "I lost a tooth in my vermouth while I was in Perth celebrating my birthday with an uncouth youth on Earth Day."

Vine Valley Vacation

Veronica was very often vexed by the provocative "V's" of the venal visiting Virginian violinist and the vindictive Venezuelan viceroy who gave viper venom vaccinations to the vulnerable villagers when they came to Vine Valley each year on vacation.

Did the meanings change as you took words out of the Braintwisters?
Will you remember to reread your documents carefully after you've edited them?
Good.

Write these concepts (three to five times each) on a separate page:

Concept #40	Concept #41	Concept #42
Murder your darlings.	Writing is a *process*, not a product.	Do one thing at a time. Write. Then organize. Then edit.

Please write your journal entry for Chapter 8 **NOW**. For instructions, see Page 7.

CHAPTER 9: EDITING FOR READERS

If you've worked diligently to this point, you know how to get things in the right order, cut out bits of nonsense you fell in love with, remove sections you don't need and get rid of anything that distracts your readers from what they need to hear.

In Chapter 9 we'll cover:

- Four important things to keep in mind while editing for an audience
- The grammar of writing for people other than you
- What to do when you run into a long, difficult-to-understand sentence
- What to do when there's not *enough* sentence or when you only have *a bit of* sentence to work with

So far in the writing process you've practiced, you've let the right side of your brain loose to create a rich, chaotic, sloppy first draft. You've considered your audience, answered their questions, moved the result you want to the top of the page and rearranged your paragraphs in a logical order.

CONCEPT #41: *Writing is a **process**—not a product.*

Now it's time to switch to left brain activity and get some seriously picky, obsessive-compulsive things done. Note that I use "picky" and "obsessive-compulsive" in the *nicest* possible way.

Some people think editing is like surgery. It's precise. It's careful. It's fun. Others think editing is like sculpture; you smooth out all the rough surfaces so that the result is good to look at and good to read. Pick your own analogy. The point is, we're going to perform an *excessectomy* to smooth out the rough spots, polish the work and get rid of any dangerous sharp edges.

I must tell you before we begin; I love this part. Just as I love the wild freedom of first drafting, I love the precision of the editing process. I love honing each sentence to its finest form. I love making murky points clear and making sure that each sentence is easy to read—that it follows the sentence before it and leads gracefully into the sentence that follows.

One of the best things about editing is that all the material (thanks to the chaotic draft I did first) is there on paper. So now I don't have to wrack my brain or wrestle with the order of things—all I have to do is spiff up what's *there already.*

CONCEPT #42:   *Do one thing at a time: Write. Then organize. Then edit.*

Just as you can't write and edit at the same time, because the two processes cancel each other out, you can't edit unless the raw material is on the page (or screen) in front of you so *all* you have to concentrate on is the polishing.

I edit to make it easy for my readers to understand what I've written quickly and easily because:

- ♦ Readers will edit if I don't.
- ♦ Readers will misunderstand if they can.
- ♦ Readers are always in a hurry.

This means that you can't make readers stop mid-sentence and go back to the beginning to untangle what you were trying to say.

When you become your own editor, you need to remember these points.

Grammar: (Don't worry. This isn't going to be like your high school English class, I promise.) Grammar exists to help you help your readers understand *exactly* what you're saying to them.

Grammar controls the "music" of the language. Often you can check your grammar by reading your document out loud. If you can't read a sentence on one breath, you should consider breaking that sentence up into two or more sentences, or see if you can phrase it another way to make it easier for your reader to understand.

I'm not giving you complex, hard-to-remember rules here; all I'm saying is, "Read the thing out loud and see if it *sounds* right." Let's start by defining the basic English sentence:

> A sentence is a group of words that contains a subject (the person or thing doing the action) and a verb (the action).
>
> A proper sentence expresses a complete thought.

Long, difficult-to-understand sentences often contain several thoughts that would be more effective if they stood alone or were broken up into different sentences. Trying to pack all your thoughts into one sentence is counterproductive.

Writing is the most effective way of putting *your* ideas directly into the minds of *other people*. It *only* works if your thoughts are easily understood. The good news is that you don't have to be Hemingway to edit well. There are several easy, mechanical ways to wrest clarity from confusion.

CONCEPT #43: *Use software to save time.*

Write these concepts (three to five times each) on a separate page:

Concept #43	Concept #44	Concept #45
Use software to save time.	Whatever's missing makes the sentence hard to understand.	Putting the right word in the right place saves time.

PUTTING BILL GATES TO WORK

Using your Word programs to help you write is one of the quickest, most convenient tools in your arsenal.

Go to the TOOLS MENU. Click on SPELLING AND GRAMMAR. Go to the bottom of the column and click OPTIONS.

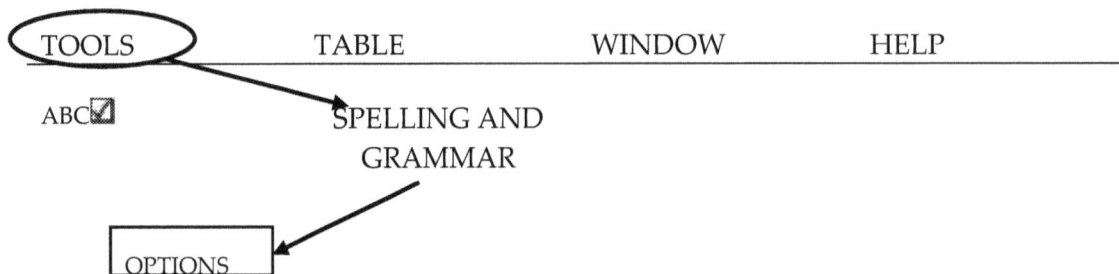

TOOLS	TABLE	WINDOW	HELP

ABC☑   SPELLING AND
                       GRAMMAR

OPTIONS

On the OPTIONS MENU, click the SPELLING & GRAMMAR tab.

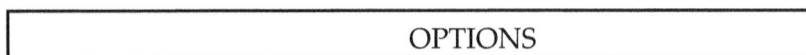

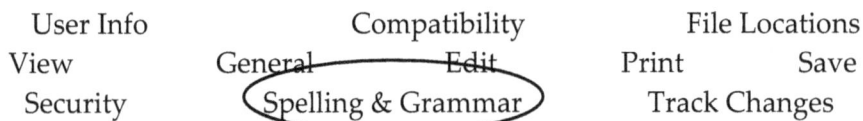

OPTIONS

User Info	Compatibility		File Locations
View	General	Edit	Print	Save
Security	Spelling & Grammar		Track Changes

Click: CHECK GRAMMAR WITH SPELLING *and* SHOW READABILITY STATISTICS boxes.

Spelling ——————————————————————————————

☑ Check spelling as you type
☑ Always suggest corrections

Grammar ————————————————————————————

☑ Check grammar as you type
☑ Check grammar with spelling
☑ Show readability statistics

Go to the bottom of the tab to the window where it says: GRAMMAR & STYLE. Click SETTINGS.

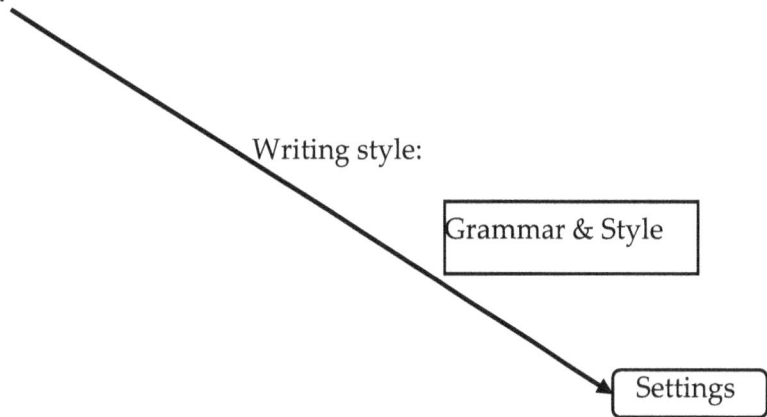

Writing style:

Grammar & Style

Settings

Check all boxes in the GRAMMAR & STYLE OPTIONS drop down window.

OPTIONS

Grammar & style options:

Grammar:
☑ Fragments and run-ons
☑ Misused words
☑ Questions
☑ Subject-verb agreement

Style:
☑ Misused words
☑ Passive sentences

Note: Using your Word programs for help or suggestions is fine, but be warned: these programs are sometimes *very wrong*. You still need to use your own judgment to make sure what you write is perfectly correct.

REVIEWING TOOLS:

TRACK CHANGES AND COMMENT BAR

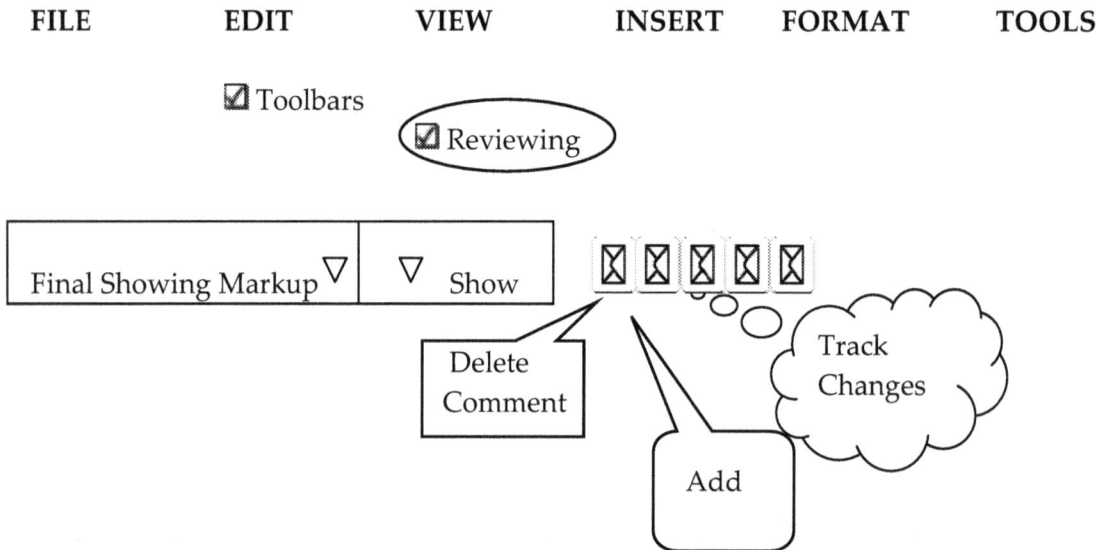

EDITING: SURGICAL APPROACH

Good editing depends on good diagnosis. So, let's look at some murky sentences and see how we can diagnose the basic idea in them mechanically:

> This <u>performance</u> has been the <u>result</u> of <u>balanced economic policies</u> and an extremely <u>favorable external environment</u>, particularly in terms of <u>US demand for Mexican</u> manufacturing <u>exports</u> (19% year to July) and <u>oil prices</u> (the Mexican oil basket is up US$8 per barrel year to August).

There are 46 words in this sentence, too many words for any reader to handle easily. You can tell how difficult to understand it is by reading it out loud. If you can't finish the sentence (out loud) on a single intake of breath, you need to look at it again to see if you can do something to make it shorter. Or clearer. We learned how to underline important words and stick them together without connectives. But, there are *other* ways to simplify a bulky sentence. Or, to flesh out a skimpy one.

Here's what to do if you're not sure if you have a complete sentence:

Ask yourself if you can turn the sentence into a Yes/No question.

All complete English sentences can be turned into questions that can be answered by "Yes" or "No." Let's test the sentence we just looked at. Here's a list of Yes/No question words to help you turn the sentence below into a yes/no question *without adding anything* but "do," "does," or "did":

YES/NO QUESTION WORDS

The question words that follow will always lead to a "yes" or "no" answer:

do	have	am	can	~~ought to~~
does	has	is	could	~~must~~
did	had	are	shall	may
		was	should	~~might~~
		were	will	
			would	

(I've crossed out some of the words because the questions they form are too formal for most business writing or speech).

"Has this <u>performance</u> been the <u>result</u> of <u>balanced economic policies</u> and an extremely <u>favorable external environment</u>, particularly in terms of <u>US demand for Mexican</u> manufacturing <u>exports</u> (19% year to July) and <u>oil prices</u> (the Mexican oil basket is up US$8 per barrel year to August? " Ask yourself:

Is this a Yes/No question? Yes. Can you break the sentence up and turn each piece into a Yes/No question? Yes. Let's try.

a) Has this performance been the result of balanced economic policies and an extremely favorable external environment? (*Have balanced economic policies and a favorable external environment caused this performance?*)
b) Is US demand for Mexican manufacturing exports up?
c) Are oil prices up?

Now, if you turn the questions back into statements, you'll have three complete, clear sentences:

a) Balanced economic policies and a favorable external environment caused this performance.
b) US demand for manufacturing exports is up (19% year to July).
c) The Mexican oil basket is up, too (US$8 per barrel year to August).

Which statement is clearer? The original 46-word sentence or the three shorter sentences?

Which version is easier to remember?

REARRANGEMENT REMEDY

Ask yourself if the sentence in question is a complete sentence or a run-on. How about the next sentence—complete or run-on?

"After three hours of heated discussion, the executive board decided to give you an enormous raise."

If you decided it was a complete sentence—bravo! Did you guess, or did you test the sentence so you knew for sure?

Here's the fail-safe three-step test to see if a sentence is complete:

FAIL-SAFE COMPLETE SENTENCE TEST

(1) Find any introductory material at the beginning of your "sentence." Move that introductory material to the end of the sentence. See arrow pointing east on the next page.

(2) Your introductory material is now at the end of the sentence.

(3) See if you can turn this new sentence into a "Yes/No" question without *deleting anything or adding anything* but "do," "does," or "did." Examine the chart below.

INTRODUCTORY MATERIAL	SUBJECT	PREDICATE (the verb and what follows it)	FORMER INTRODUCTORY MATERIAL
(1) (After three hours of heated discussion)	the executive board	decided to give you an enormous raise.	
	The executive board	decided to give you an enormous raise	**(2)** (after three hours of heated discussion.)
(3) Did	~~T~~the executive board	decided~~ ~~ to give you an enormous raise	(after three hours of heated discussion?)

CHECK YOUR OWN WRITING

Ask yourself the following questions for each group of words that starts with a capital letter and ends with a period:

Step 1.   *Does it begin with a group of words that can be moved to the end of the sentence without changing meaning? If it can, move that word group to the end.*

Step 2.   *Can you make a Yes/No question without deleting or adding anything but "do," "does," or " did?" If so, it is a sentence.*

Step 3.   *If it doesn't turn into a yes/no question:*

      a. Can it be hooked into a neighboring sentence?
      b. Do you need to add something to it?
      c. Do you need to take something out?

Step 4.   *If you need to add something or take something out, start over again at step 2.*

> Some sentences don't have any introductory material. Not to worry. Just start at step 2 by turning the sentence into a Yes/No question.

All right, how does the Yes/No question method work on a sentence like this?

"Once that pool is defined we are able to break out the moneys the way we would like, but the overall pool is determined by the Business Unit report card (not by individual lines of business within the business unit) which is designated by GLT."

a)   **Are** we able to break out the moneys the way we would like, once that pool is defined?

b)   **Is** the overall pool determined by the Business Unit report card?

c)   **Are** individual lines of business within the business unit designated by GLT?

Now turn the questions back into statements and what have we got?

"Once that pool is defined, we'll be able to break out the moneys the way we'd like. The overall pool is determined by the Business Unit report card, but the individual lines of business within the business unit are designated by the GLT."

REVIEWING THE FORMULA

If there is introductory material at the beginning of the sentence, move it to the end.

If there is no introductory material at the beginning of the sentence, simply form a Yes/No question with the sentence. If the sentence is long, handle its other elements by turning them into individual Yes/No questions. Turn all your questions back into statements.

SENTENCE STRUCTURE: RUN-ONS

One of the writing problems I run into most frequently is the problem of *run-on sentences* (sentences that are a little *more* than proper sentences) and *sentence fragments* (sentences that are little *less* than proper sentences).

Note: I'm using "everyday" words rather than grammatical terms so you can use them without learning an entirely new vocabulary.

Writers frequently write run-on sentences when they're excited about something or when they just want to get the writing part over with quickly. Run-on sentences make readers confused and force them to reread what you've written.

RUN-ON SENTENCE EXAMPLES

Here are two of my recent run-on favorites:

1. In my previous companies I read a lot of memos from management with references to seminars, professional meetings, birthday parties, parties for colleagues from England, Germany, charity donations, popular movies and TV programs recommended by management.

2. Have you ever thought of working with a quick-thinking, go-get-'em creative team of entrepreneurs, being able to do what you think is the proper thing to do when you want to do it without getting permission from your boss?

My grammarian friends will accuse me of cheating here, but I feel if you can't read a sentence on one breath, that sentence is bound to be a run-on. Try reading sentences 1 and 2 in one breath, and you'll see what I mean.

Often, run-on sentences are two sentences that are incorrectly joined. Example sentence 2 falls into that category. If you separate its two parts, you'll have (a) one complete sentence and (b) one sentence fragment:

(a)   Have you ever thought of working with a quick-thinking, go-get-'em creative team of entrepreneurs?

(b)   Being able to do what you think is the proper thing to do when you want to do it without getting permission from your boss?

We know example (a) is a complete sentence (an independent clause) because it starts with a capital letter, ends with a question mark, has a subject and a verb and expresses one complete thought. Independent clauses are very strong and can stand all by themselves. That's why they're called "independent."

Sentence fragments can't stand alone. They're missing something. What is sentence (b) missing? Once you've found out, rewrite it (on a separate sheet of paper) so it's complete. **Do it NOW.**

Did your rewrite look like this?

 Have you longed to do what you think is right (when you want to) without getting permission from your boss?

What about example 1?

"In my previous companies I read a lot of memos from management with references to seminars, professional meetings, birthday parties, parties for colleagues from England, Germany, charity donations, popular movies and TV programs recommended by management."

Can you find the complete sentence in the example on page 106? If so, write it here.

If you put a period after the word "management," in the first line, how would you rewrite the sentence fragment that remains? Write your rewrite on a separate piece of paper.

SENTENCE FRAGMENTS: OOOPS, NOT ENOUGH SENTENCE

A fragment is a *piece* of a sentence, a snippet, not a *complete* sentence. We use fragments every day in both informal and formal speech. Newspaper headlines use lots of sentence fragments:

"President Over Barrel"
"First Lady Divorce Delay"
"Crown Prince's Steamy Affair"

Professional writers use incomplete sentences occasionally, but watch it— fragments are frowned on in business writing.

Advertising, which uses fragments liberally, has destroyed our natural sense of the completeness or incompleteness of most sentences causing fragments look normal to us. I use fragments all the time. To make a point. To emphasize an attitude. To wake my reader up. See?

As a rule, a sentence fragment is a piece of a sentence that's missing something vital. Maybe it's a subject (the person or thing doing the action) maybe it's a verb (the action itself).

FIXING SENTENCE FRAGMENTS

CONCEPT #44: *Whatever's missing makes the sentence difficult to understand.*

This sentence fragment is missing a verb:

The American vampire, difficult to understand but fun to live with.

The test for fragments is the same as the test for run-ons. Can you turn the sentence into a yes/no question?

a)   *Is* the American vampire difficult to understand but fun to live with?

The question itself will tell you what's missing. In this example, it's the verb "is." The verb shows up in the question, but not the original fragment. If you put "is" into the fragment (example b) you'll make it into a complete sentence.

"The American vampire is difficult to understand but fun to live with."

Here are some fragments to practice with.

SENTENCE FRAGMENT EXERCISE

1.   The Hendersens failed to realize. That gerbils may be arguing when they snap at each other.

2.   The Floridian gecko being the only lizard that is as distinctive as, or more distinctive than, my cousin's ex-husband.

3.   Her significant other having an enormous CD collection of Heavy Metal music.

4.   Have you seen the rattled rabbit? Hopping in its rabbit hutch.

5.   Equipment that also produces new ways to better exploit the target market.

6.   Dr. Marcus a kind of bargain-basement guru.

7.   Colored precious gemstones found 20-feet deep in the Emerald City of Oz.

'8.   Alaskan three-toed sloths not to be confused with Virginian two-toed sloths.

9.   Never having seen a wall-size TV before. The aborigines thought it was an instrument of torture.

10.   New York rents are being lowered. Because of the property owners' kindness and generosity.

ANSWER KEY: SENTENCE FRAGMENT EXERCISE

1. The Hendersens failed to realize that gerbils may be arguing when they snap at each other. *(Combine both clauses into one sentence.)*
2. The Floridian gecko is the only lizard that is as distinctive as, or more distinctive than, my cousin's ex-husband.
3. Her significant other has an enormous CD collection of Heavy Metal music.
4. Have you seen the rattled rabbit hopping in its rabbit hutch? *(Combine both clauses into one sentence.)*
5. This is equipment that also produces new ways to better exploit the target market.
6. Dr. Marcus is a kind of bargain-basement guru.
7. Colored precious gemstones are found 20-feet deep in the Emerald City of Oz.
8. Alaskan three-toed to sloths are not to be confused with Virginian two-toed sloths.
9. Never having seen a wall-size TV before, the aborigines thought it was an instrument of torture. *(Combine both clauses into one sentence.)*
10. New York rents are being lowered because of the property owners' kindness and generosity. *(Combine both clauses into one sentence.)*

MOVING MISPLACED MODIFIERS

What's wrong with this sentence?

"I will take care of the catering which must be arranged for the meeting in August."

Are the *meetings* in August, or must the *catering* be done in August, or is it the *arranging* that needs to be done in August? Do you know what the answer is? Well, neither do I. Creating this confusion is called: misplacing a modifier. Readers who get lost re-read the sentence and call or e-mail the author to find out what's really going on. If you'd rather not be bothered with these calls and e-mails, don't misplace your modifiers.

CONCEPT #45: *Putting the right word in the right place saves time.*

Grammarians amuse themselves collecting lists of misplaced modifiers that completely change the meaning of the message. Here are four examples to help you recognize what a misplaced modifier looks and sounds like:

a. *He smacked the dog because it chewed up his shoe with a newspaper.*

b. *Mark and Sue gave their daughter a doll that's so lifelike it wets its pants for Christmas.*

c. *The SUV passed me as I walked down the street at sixty miles an hour.*

d. *You are welcome to visit the cemetery where famous Russian and soviet composers, artists, and writers are buried daily except Thursday.*

FINDING WHERE MODIFIERS BELONG–THE EASY WAY

The best way to avoid misplacing modifiers is to keep them as close as possible to the words they modify. You can do this by asking yourself these questions:

WHO? WHAT? WHEN? WHERE? WHY? HOW?

In example (a) What did he smack the dog with? *A newspaper.* Put *with a newspaper* next to "He smacked the dog" and you've un-confused both sentence and reader by writing: *"He smacked the dog with a newspaper because it chewed up his shoe."*

Now try fixing examples (b) and (c) and (d) by yourself.

ANSWER KEY: MOVING MISPLACED MODIFIERS

a.   *He smacked the dog **with a newspaper** because it chewed up his shoe.*

b.   *Mark and Sue gave their daughter a doll **for Christmas** that's so lifelike it wets its pants.*

c.   *The SUV passed me **at 60 miles an hour** as I walked down the street.*

d.   *You are welcome to visit the cemetery **(daily except Thursday)** where famous Russian and soviet composers, artists, and writers are buried.*

GETTING YOUR SUBJECTS AND VERBS TO AGREE

One of the problems I run into frequently is the mismatching of subjects and verbs. I'm constantly testing my sentences because, although I hate to admit it, if my subjects and verbs don't match I look careless or uneducated or both. Everyone falls into the mis-match trap from time to time. Consider Example 1 below.

1.   The purchase <u>order</u> for the new lab rats *have* been approved.

I've underlined the subject and italicized the verb in this sentence to illustrate how easy it is to lose track of things.

The person who wrote the sentence (okay, *I* wrote the sentence) saw the word "rats," decided that "rats" was a plural noun—and instantly put in a plural verb (have) to match. The problem is that "rats" is *not* the subject of this sentence—the *purchase order* is. "Order" is singular, so it needs a singular verb to complement it. Let's try another sentence.

1.   <u>Each</u> of the Romans *agree* with the banquet arrangements.

"*Each*" really means "each *one*." One is singular. Since the verb "agree" refers to "each <u>one</u>" it needs to be third person singular, e.g., "each one agrees." How about this sentence?

2.   Multiple terrorist surveillance sites, although giving us some geographical flexibility, causes confusion among the commanding officers.

In Example 2, two things have probably caused the subject/verb disagreement problem. The first is that the writer has misidentified "*flexibility*" as the subject. The second is that the amount of intervening material, "*although giving us some geographical flexibility*" has caused the writer to forget about the real subject ("*sites*") entirely.

Getting around trouble in subject/verb agreement is easy when you check to see that every singular subject matches every singular verb. The same advice goes for plural subjects and plural verbs. Remember, this happens *only* during the editing phase of the writing process. None of this matters when you're doing your first draft.

MAKING SURE YOUR PRONOUNS MATCH THE NOUNS THEY REPRESENT

A noun's a person, place or thing. A pronoun's a word that *stands in* for that person place or thing so you don't end up repeating yourself.

Here's a problem sentence: *"There will be a Moscow exhibition of arts by 15,000 Soviet Republic painters and sculptors; these were executed over the past two years."* Please figure out what's wrong, then fix the sentence.

The noun is *"arts"* the pronoun is *"these."* The problem with the sentence is that "painters and sculptors" are also nouns and they appear so close to *"these"* that you're led to believe that the arts on view are the product of *painters and sculptors* who were recently shot by a firing squad.

Always check your writing to see that your nouns and your pronouns match. You wouldn't wear a polka dot shirt with plaid pants, would you? Never mind. Just make sure your nouns match your pronouns.

CONCEPT #46: *Keep your eye on the nouns.*

COMPLEX SENTENCES: PUTTING YOUR MOST IMPORTANT IDEA LAST

Take the complex sentence: *"As Rudolf was eating breakfast, Marla began writing her novel."* Which action do you think is most important to the writer—Rudolf's eating breakfast, or Marla's beginning her novel?

You don't have to guess; you can tell from the way the sentence is constructed that the writer thought the novel writing was more important than the breakfast eating. Why? Because it comes last in the sentence. If the writer thought the breakfasting was the most important of the two actions, the sentence would have read like this: *"Marla began writing her novel as Rudolf was eating breakfast."*

Figure out what's most important to *you* in the following sentences, then adjust the sentences to reflect that importance. **Do it NOW.**

1. Because they were ignoring Boris, Sheila dropped the Ming vase.
2. As soon as Iggy debuts at Carnegie Hall, Isaac Stern will leave for Paris.
3. If you'll write us on company stationery, we'll send you the most recent editions.
4. As soon as the rainy season is over, we'll go to Bambara.
5. When you come to the third Starbuck's, turn left.

CONCEPT #47: *Put the most important point at the end.*

Write these concepts (three to five times each) on a separate page:

Concept #46	Concept #47	Concept #48
Keep an eye on the nouns.	Put the most important point at the end.	Lunchroom, lunchroom, lunchroom.

Write your journal entry for Chapter 9 **NOW.** For instructions, see Page 7.

Your Notes Here

CHAPTER 10: LUNCHROOMING

Lunchrooming? What is *lunchrooming*? It's my way of turning corporate-speak into human-speak—the easy way. This is how the term "lunchrooming" came about:

I was teaching a writing class to the salespeople at a large publishing company. We got to the part where I explain that big words and passive voice sentences were hard to remember. The way to fix the problem, I said, was to look at what you'd written (the stuff that was full of big words and passive voice sentences) then close your eyes and imagine how you'd express the same idea to a friend over lunch.

When for example, was the last time you used the word "implementing" or "paradigm" or "competencies" or the phrase "it has come to my attention," when you were having lunch with a friend?

At this point, a woman in the back of the room said, "Oh, I get it, you want us to *lunchroom*." That's how the verb "lunchroom" was born. The idea is: the clearest words are often the shortest words and the most complicated ideas can be best expressed in simple sentences.

A speechwriter for Franklin D. Roosevelt wrote:

"We are endeavoring to construct an inclusive society."

Roosevelt looked at the line and instantly revised it to read:

"We are trying to build a country where no one is left out."

If FDR lunchroomed, so can you.

In the exercises that follow, I'm going to ask you to do the same thing.

LUNCHROOMING EXERCISE #1:

Please read through numbers 1 through 4. They all belong in one paragraph. Once you've read them, lunchroom them so that they are easy to read and they make sense. *Write your lunchroomed sentences in the spaces under the originals. Be sure to read all the original sentences before you begin writing. Read for the main idea. Then, isolate the major problem management is having. Identify (or invent) what's causing the problem. Encourage the appropriate people to solve the problem.*

Transhumance Incorporated

Memo

To: Supply Department   From: Debbie Fertig

1.   It has come to my attention that an uncomfortable independence is becoming part of our organization's supply department.

2.   The Company believes that everyone should cooperate in reaching our common goals.

3.   We encourage employees to be proactive in selling our products to the best of their abilities.

4.   I appreciate your cooperation in ensuring that our staff has the proper equipment.

ANSWER KEY: LUNCHROOMING EXERCISE #1:

Transhumance, Inc.

Memo

To: *The Supply Department*   From: *Debbie Fertig*

1.   *The sales force and the PR Department tell me they're having difficulty getting the samples they need from the Supply Department.*

2.   *I've always believed teamwork is the most important part of getting where we want to be in the Interspecies communication industry.*

3.   *So I'd like each of you to work as closely as you can with your colleagues to give them the supplies they need so they can demonstrate our equipment in the best way possible.*

4.   *Thanks for making sure our staff has an ample supply of samples.*

LUNCHROOMING EXERCISE # 2:

There is a movement in England called, "The Plain English Campaign." Its purpose is to show how even the most complicated language can be simplified. Sentences 1 through 4 on the next page come from the Plain English Website.

http://www.plainenglish.co.uk/index.html (Plain English Campaign Home Page)

http://www.plainenglish.co.uk/A-Z.html   (A-Z alternative words)

http://www.plainenglish.co.uk/guides.html (Free guides)

DIRECTIONS: Please read each of the sentences below. Turn your eyes away. Get the sense of what each sentence is saying. Then, lunchroom that sentence. Write your answer in the space below the original sentence.

1. High-quality learning environments are a necessary precondition for facilitation and enhancement of the ongoing learning process.

2. If there are any points on which you require explanation or further particulars, we shall be glad to furnish such additional details as may be required by telephone.

3. It is important that you shall read the notes, advice and information detailed opposite, then complete the form overleaf (all sections) prior to its immediate return to the council by way of the envelope provided.

4. Your inquiry about the use of the entrance area at the library for the purpose of displaying posters and leaflets about Welfare and Supplementary benefit rates, gives rise to the question of the provenance and authoritativeness of the material to be displayed. Posters and leaflets issued by the Central Office of Information, the Department of Health and Social Security and other authoritative bodies are usually displayed in the library, but items of a disputatious or polemic kind, while not necessarily excluded, are considered individually.

ANSWER KEY: LUNCHROOMING EXERCISE #2

1. *People need good schools if they are to learn properly.*

2. *If you have any questions, please call.*

3. *Please read the notes opposite before you fill in the form. Then send it back to us as soon as possible in the enclosed envelope.*

4. *Thank you for your letter asking permission to put up posters in the entrance area of the library. Before we can give you an answer, we will need to see a copy of the posters to make sure they won't offend anyone.*

LUNCHROOMING AND STYLE

The more you lunchroom, the more you'll develop a personal style. Until your own style emerges, you may be interested in copying someone else's. My philosophy on copying other people's style is: I'm all in favor of it.

When I was just beginning to write, I copied everyone from Dorothy Parker to Dostoyevsky. Those were the authors I enjoyed reading, and theirs was a rhythm I felt comfortable with. As time went on, I copied less. My own style developed, and now I write in a voice that is genuinely my own. We all have to start somewhere, and copying the style of someone you respect isn't a bad place to start.

Parodies are often written mimicking a popular style. Here's an example, written in typical press release style:

MCCHEESE ANNOUNCES AMBITIOUS INTERNATIONAL PLAN

McCheese, with its 900 restaurants devoted to cheese fondue, has an ambitious plan for its future.

With the opening of a restaurant in Tokyo, Japan, next week, McCheese starts an international expansion of its operations that will lead to the creation of 200 new restaurants in the next five years.

The growth of the company is based on the principle of the "3Cs": community involvement, cultural integration and cheese production.

Community involvement is a concept created by Peter Stilton, CEO of McCheese.

Each McCheese restaurant is involved in the life of the country, the city or the town where it is located. The new Tokyo restaurant, for example, will sponsor Japan's annual Sumo wrestling competition. The New York restaurant will donate 1% of its revenue to the "Bench in Central Park" project.

The second key concept is cultural integration. The menu of each McCheese restaurant will reflect the culinary roots of the region in which it is situated. In Maine, McCheese will offer lobster fondue; in New Mexico, jalapeño chili fondue; in San Francisco's Chinatown, Peking Duck fondue. The last of the three C's is the basic element of the fondue itself: cheese.

This February, McCheese will introduce its own cheese, which will be produced in Vermont in the most up-to-date facilities. The preliminary taste testing results have been more than satisfying. McCheese's test cheese won this year's prestigious Granny Award in the category: Best New Food Event of the Year.

McCheese is very proud to have been called: "The most innovative company in America," by *The Wall Street Journal*, and with its new strategy, expects to gain millions more satisfied customers.

Two parody websites that are worth a look:

http://www.mindcrystals.com/ and
http://www.dearauntnettie.com/museum/index.htm

Please write your journal entry for Chapter 10 **NOW**. For instructions, see Page 7.

CHAPTER 11: GIVING GOOD GRAMMAR

Talk about grammar and everyone starts to fidget and look at the clock. Nothing stops conversation quite as dead as a grammar question. Everyone, *everyone,* is terminally insecure about his or her ability to tell a noun from a pronoun or an adjective from an adverb. You don't need to know anything about grammar to use this review because you'll find the answers on the pages that follow. Whew!

First let's see what you know; then we'll fill in the blanks together.

A noun is	
An article is	
A pronoun is	
An adjective is	
A verb is	
An adverb is	
A (grammatical) subject is	

A preposition is	
An object is	
A phrase is	
A clause is	
The "active voice" is	
The "passive voice" is	
A prefix is	
A suffix is	
A sentence fragment is	
A run-on sentence is	

How did you do? Check yourself against the answer key on the next several pages.

ANSWER KEY: GRAMMAR REVIEW

A noun is	a person, place, thing or idea. An actor, a movie house, a camcorder and a plotline are all nouns.
An article is	*a, an* or *the.* Articles announce nouns that follow them.
A pronoun is	a word that stands in for a noun. *She, he, it* or *they* are pronouns.
An adjective is	a word that describes a noun. *Fuzzy, silky* or *delicious* are adjectives.
A verb is	an action or a state of being. *Jog, warble, be* are verbs.
An adverb is	a word that describes a verb, an adjective or another adverb. *Correctly, beautifully, very* are adverbs.
A (grammatical) subject is	the person or thing doing the action. *Jimmy* goes bungee jumping, *Guy* snores, *Maryanne* is double jointed. *Jimmy, Guy* and *Maryanne* are grammatical subjects.
A preposition is	a word that expresses:
remember "position" and you'll remember pre*position*	✓ direction: *to, into, across, toward* ✓ time: *before, after, during, until* ✓ figurative locations: *for, against, with.*

An object is	the person or thing receiving the action. John threw the *hunting knife.*
A phrase is	a group of words *without* a verb. *The town gardener* is a phrase. *In the winter* and *during the summer* are phrases, too.
A clause is	a group of words *with* a verb. *Charles embraced the town gardener* is a clause.
The "active voice" is	a grammatical term for writing that tells you who's doing what to whom. *Hepsibah made mistakes* is written in the active voice.
The "passive voice" is	a grammatical term for writing that leaves out the "who" part. *Mistakes were made* is written in the passive voice. *Mistakes were made by Hepsibah,* is written in the passive voice, too. It includes the "who" part, but puts it at the end of the sentence.
A prefix is	a specific group of letters that can be attached to the *beginning* of a word to change its meaning. Comfortable becomes–*un*comfortable or matter becomes *anti*matter.

A suffix is	a specific group of letters that can be attached to the *end* of a word to change its grammatical form. Beauty is a noun. Beauti*ful* is an adjective. Drive is a verb. Dri*ver* is a noun. –ful and –er are suffixes.
A sentence is	a group of words that begins with a capital letter, ends with a period, or a question mark, contains a subject and a verb and conveys a single idea. *The bat hung upside down in the closet.* *Whose bat hung upside down in the closet?*
A sentence fragment is	an incomplete sentence in which something crucial is missing. *"Having slain the Jabberwock,"* is a sentence fragment.
A run-on sentence is	two or more sentences that are fused without the proper punctuation to separate them. *"Once I had an imaginary friend he lived inside my toothbrush,"* is a run-on sentence.

If you're still insecure in the grammar area, check into the Michigan University Grammar Website for lengthier explanations. Here's the address:

http://www-personal.umich.edu/~laubenth/writing/grammar.htm

PERVERSE RULES OF ENGLISH GRAMMAR

The list of rules on the next pages has come to me in pieces over the Internet for the last number of years, so it is a collection from various sources—most of them anonymous. Or so I thought, until I ran across this book:

How Not to Write: The Essential Misrules of Grammar by William Safire.

It's fun to read and offers concrete, easy to digest, explanations about why English grammar works the way it does. I highly recommend it. The following section is from HOW NOT TO WRITE by William Safire. Copyright © 1990 by Cobbett Corporation. Used by permission of W. W. Norton & Company, Inc.

The idea of making a mistake while laying down rules ("Thimk," and "We Never Make Misteaks") has amused English teachers for decades. Each of the rules below *demonstrates the mistake it wants you to avoid.* Try your hand at correcting these very odd grammar rules:

1. Avoid run-on sentences they are hard to read.

2. Don't use no double negatives.

3. Remember to never split an infinitive.

4. The passive voice is to be avoided.

5. Use the semicolon properly, always use it where it is appropriate; and never where it isn't.

6. Reserve the apostrophe for it's proper use and omit it when its not needed.

7. If any word is improper at the end of a sentence, a linking verb is.

8. Never use repetitive redundancies.

9. Everyone should be careful to use a singular pronoun with singular nouns in their writing.

10. If I've told you once, I've told you a thousand times, resist hyperbole.

11. Always pick on the correct idiom.

12. "Avoid overuse of 'quotation "marks.""

13. The adverb always follows the verb.

14. Do not put statements in the negative form.

15. Avoid alliteration. Always.

16. Prepositions are not words to end sentences with.

17. Verbs has to agree with their subjects.

18. No sentence fragments.

19. Eschew ampersands & abbreviations, etc.

20. Avoid commas, that are not necessary.

21. Eliminate quotations. As Ralph Waldo Emerson said, "I hate quotations. Tell me what you know."

22. Avoid clichés like the plague. (They're old hat.)

23. Employ the vernacular.

24. Comparisons are as bad as clichés.

25. If you reread your work, you will find on rereading that a great deal of repetition can be avoided by rereading and editing.

26. A writer must not shift your point of view.

27. And don't start a sentence with a conjunction.

28. Understatement is always best.

29. One-word sentences? Eliminate.

30. Don't overuse exclamation marks!!!

31. Be more or less specific.

32. Analogies in writing are like feathers on a snake.

33. Place pronouns as close as possible, especially in long sentences, as of ten or more words, to their antecedents.

34. Even if a mixed metaphor sings, it should be derailed.

35. Hyphenate between syllables and avoid un-necessary hyphens.

36. Who needs rhetorical questions?

37. Write all adverbial forms correct.

38. Exaggeration is a billion times worse than understatement.

39. Don't be redundant; don't use more words than necessary; it's highly superfluous.

40. Proofread carefully to see if you any words out.

ANSWER KEY: PERVERSE RULES OF ENGLISH GRAMMAR

1. Avoid run-on sentences. They are hard to read.
2. Don't use double negatives.
3. Remember never to split an infinitive.
4. Avoid the passive voice.
5. Use the semicolon properly; always use it where it is appropriate and never where it isn't.
6. Reserve the apostrophe for its proper use and omit it when it's not needed.
7. A linking verb is improper at the end of a sentence.
8. Don't repeat yourself.
9. Everyone should be careful to use a singular pronoun with a singular noun in his or her writing.
10. Resist hyperbole.
11. Always pick the correct idiom.
12. Avoid overusing quotation marks.
13. The adverb sometimes follows the verb.
14. Avoid putting statements in the negative form.
15. Steer clear of alliteration.
16. Prepositions are not words with which to end sentences.
17. Verbs have to agree with their subjects.
18. Avoid writing sentence fragments.

19.   Eschew ampersands and abbreviations.
20.   Avoid unnecessary commas.
21.   Eliminate quotations.
22.   Avoid clichés.
23.   Use everyday language.
24.   Avoid comparisons.
25.   Reread and edit your copy so you don't repeat yourself.
26.   A writer must not shift his or her point of view.
27.   Don't start a sentence with a conjunction.
28.   Understatement is best.
29.   Eliminate one-word sentences.
30.   Don't overuse exclamation marks!
31.   Be specific.
32.   Avoid clumsy analogies.
33.   Place pronouns as close as possible to their antecedents especially in long sentences.
34.   Avoid mixed metaphors.
35.   Hyphenate between syl-
      lables and avoid unnecessary hyphens.
36.   Avoid rhetorical questions.
37.   Write all adverbial forms correctly.
38.   Exaggeration is worse than understatement.
39.   Don't be redundant.
40.   Proofread carefully to see if you have left any words out.

> Which "rules" do you break all the time?
> Write them on a separate sheet of paper. **NOW.**

ADDING SYLLABLES AND CUTTING WORDS

Interestingly enough, an added syllable can change the meaning or function of a word and in the process, shorten a sentence. Prefixes are syllables attached to the beginning of words. Comfortable/*un*comfortable, and done/*re*done, are examples. Syllables attached to ends of words such as rust/rust*y*, tact/tact*less,* pain/pain*ful* are called suffixes.

PREFIXES

You'd be amazed how handy prefix syllables such as *un, re,* and *mis* can be in getting rid of extra words. Look at these examples:

1. Melanie left her report **before she could finish it.**

    Melanie left her report unfinished. (5 saved words)

2. Peter Ellison gave his editor the novel **he'd written over again**.

    Peter Ellison gave his editor the rewritten novel. (4 saved words)

3. Irma Sexhour looked at her name, which **was spelled wrongly**.

    Irma Sexhour looked at her misspelled name. (4 saved words)

Can you think of any other examples where prefixes get rid of extra words? Write them here. **Do it NOW.**

SUFFIXES

Suffixes such *as ly, ment, ful, less* work well, too. Can you cut the extra words in these sentences and replace them with suffixes? **Do it NOW.**

1. For years the Whirligig Corporation had been managed in a competent way.

2. Her Royal Highness waited for the job interview at Western Thingamajigs in an impatient fashion.

3. Without doubt our customer will find out that our statement is not correct.

4. It was very fortunate that no one was in the ballroom when the avenging angel arrived.

5. She had a face that was full of beauty.

6. Kevin eyed his real estate broker with a look that had no pity.

ANSWER KEY: SUFFIXES

1. For years the Whirligig Corporation had been competently managed.
2. Her Royal Highness waited impatiently for the job interview at Western Thingamajigs.
3. Doubtless our customer will find that our statement is incorrect.
4. Fortunately, no one was in the ballroom when the avenging angel arrived.
5. She had a beautiful face.
6. Kevin eyed his real estate broker with a pitiless look.

NOUNS VS. ADJECTIVES AND ADVERBS

If you've ever played "Paper, Scissors, Rock" you'll realize that some things are stronger than others. Nouns, for example, are much stronger than adjectives because nouns are where the information is. Names, places, and things are all described by nouns. It's possible to tell an entire story by just using nouns. If I say, *"storm, lightning, barn, fire"* you know exactly what happened. If on the other hand I say *"raging, electric, red, hot"* you have no idea what went on.

MEMORY TRIGGER POEM

I found this poem on a scrap of paper, tucked in a book at the New York Public Library. I don't know the author's name, or where the poem comes from. It is, however, the best brief explanation of the parts of speech I've ever seen.

> A **noun's** a person, place, or thing,
> Or sometimes even time, like spring.
> A **verb** tells what the subject does,
> Like "jumps" or "fishes," "is" or "was."
> An **adjective** describes a noun,
> Like "gay" or "ugly," "rich" or "brown."
> An **adverb** tells you how or when,
> Like "quietly" or "well" or "then."
> A **pronoun** takes the noun's own place,
> Like "they" for "children," "she" for "Grace."
> A **preposition** leads a noun:
> "In bed," "at sea," or "to the town."
> **Conjunctions** are a bridge across
> Two sentences: "but," "and," "because."
> The **interjections**, last of all,
> *Like "Oh!" And "Ouch!" are very small.*

REPLACING NOUNS WITH VERBS

On the next page, you'll find a list of lackluster nouns people often use instead of using their more powerful verb form equivalents. Look at the nouns in Column A (on the next page) and see if you can change those nouns into verbs. Write the verbs in Column B.

Column A (Nouns)	COLUMN B (VERBS)
advice	
choice	
explosive	
integration	
investor	
maturation	
meeting	
payment	
producer	
punctuation	
rejection	
reproduction	
saturation	
signature	
solution	
stimulation	
thought	
transmission	

ANSWER KEY: REPLACING NOUNS WITH VERBS

Column A (Nouns)	Column B (Verbs)
advice	advise
choice	choose
explosive	explode
integration	integrate
investor	invest
maturation	mature
meeting	meet
payment	pay
producer	produce
punctuation	punctuate
rejection	reject
reproduction	reproduce
saturation	saturate
signature	sign
solution	solve
stimulation	stimulate
thought	think
transmission	transmit

Please write your journal entry for Chapter 11 **NOW.** For instructions, see Page 7.

CHAPTER 12: BUILDING SOLID SENTENCES

If you want to write, you'll want to write sentences. And, if you write sentences, you'll want to write them right, right? So let's recap some definitions

"A sentence is a group of words that begins with capital letter, ends with a period (or question mark) contains a subject and a verb and expresses a single complete thought."

The essential parts of a sentence are the subject (*the thing or person doing the action*) and the verb (*the action itself*).

The **subject** is usually *what* or *whom* the sentence is talking about:

Arnie went bankrupt.
The *gesture* amazed her.
Heather shredded her credit cards.
His *wife* howled nightly.
She showed her pink slip to everyone.
Gregori bit the mailperson.
The *gecko* croaked.

The **verb** is the action:

Otis *grovelled.*
He *kissed* the hem of her cloak.
The princess *escaped* last Thursday.
Abigail *spat* regularly.
The weatherman *drank.*
Posey *gave* me an enormous earache.

Most English sentences start with the *subject,* continue with a *verb* and sometimes throw in an *object.*

An **object** is something or someone who receives the action. Here are some objects:

Norberto threw the crown *jewels.*

Norberto is the subject, *threw* is the verb, *jewels* is the object.

Another way to think about constructing English sentences is the question, "Who did what to whom?"

Brunhilde slept with Martin.

(who?) Brunhilde *(did what?)* slept with *(to whom?)* Martin.

We can get fancy about it: *"The intolerable Brunhilde, Queen of the refrigerator magnets, reluctantly slept with Martin, the impossible troglodyte."* The grammatical story remains the same. The construction pattern is still: subject—verb—object.

Let's see what happens when we reverse the standard sentence order and put the object in the first position.

Mistakes were made
Bribes were accepted
The crown *jewels* were thrown by Norberto.

In the first two sentences, we have no idea who's doing the action. In the third sentence, we only find out that Norberto is doing the throwing at the end.

Which construction is easier for you to follow, subject-verb-object, or object-verb (subject)?

Why? **Write your answer here:**

Pease write five subject–verb–object sentences:

1.

2.

3.

4.

5.

Now write five sentences where the object comes first:

6.

7.

8.

9.

10.

Can you tell the difference between the two types of sentences?

Which sentences are clearer (1 through 5) or (6 through 10)?

Which sentences are briefer (1 through 5) or (6 through 10)?

Which sentences are easier to write?

What will you do with this information? Write your answer on a separate sheet of paper.

STATEMENTS AND QUESTIONS

Statements are written in subject—verb order. **Questions** start with a *question word* followed by the subject. Here are some examples of statements turned into questions:

Yasu **is** devastatingly handsome.   (statement)

Is Yasu devastatingly handsome?   (question)

The Amzallag boys **are** coming to the concert.   (statement)

Are the Amzallag boys coming to the concert?   (question)

You **have** already had the monkey-brain entrée.   (statement)

Have you already had the monkey-brain entrée?   (question)

INFORMATION QUESTION WORDS

If you want *information*, there are only six question words you need:

who
what
when
where
why
how

Reporters always try to answer as many information questions as they can in the first paragraph. That way, if the rest of the story gets cut for space, the essential information stays intact.

Please write two questions for each of the information question words above. Start your questions with the question word you're working on. Write all your questions on a separate piece of paper. **Do it NOW.**

AGREEMENT

Business writers often have trouble with agreement—not agreement between people or departments–but agreement between subjects and verbs. The rule of thumb is: if you have a *singular* subject such as:

poetry
art
Michael Bloomberg
the museum
the river
the house
coffee
independence

you must have a *singular* verb to agree with it. For example:

Martian **poetry is** unintelligible.

Michael **Bloomberg makes** politics look easy.

The **museum houses** the best Egyptian collection on the East Coast.

Coffee is best when it's strong.

Independence makes all the difference.

Just as a singular subject calls for singular verb, a *plural* subject calls for a *plural* verb. Here are some plural subjects:

tourists	department stores	the Smith-Meades
wizards	ice skating rinks	intelligent people
minstrels	seagulls	sailboats

These sentences have plural verbs that match the plural subjects:

All the **tourists say** Oaxaca is a great place to visit.

Arnoulf's **wizards** won't **use** their wands.

Minstrels always **stroll** through the Square at twilight.

Bloomingdale's, Macy's and Nordstrom's are all department stores.

Skating **rinks need** Zamboni machines to clear the ice.

The **Smith-Meades live** in Upsala.

Three of Paolo's **passions were** literature, large English sheepdogs, and Victorian corsets.

Look for mismatched subjects and verbs in the last three pieces of correspondence you've written. Did you find any? Now check the correspondence that's come over your desk in the last two weeks–any mismatches there? Can you fix them? **Do it NOW.**

The following exercises will help you test how good you are at recognizing singular/plural subjects and the verbs that match them. Beware, they look deceptively easy.

SUBJECT—VERB AGREEMENT EXERCISES

DIRECTIONS: Place a check mark next to each sentence you think is correct.

1.   There were many B-movie stars in the rehearsal hall.

2.   There was many B-movie stars in the rehearsal hall.

3.   The children in that family are adorable.

4.   The children in that family is adorable.

5.   Everybody usually watch the girls in Brazilian bikinis on the beach.

6.   Everybody usually watches the girls in Brazilian bikinis on the beach.

7.   Lorena also needs to cut her sentences shorter.

8.   Lorena also need to cut her sentences shorter.

9.   He is playing poker better because he wants to break the bank.

10.   He is playing poker better because he want to break the bank.

11.   The breeds include: spaniel, terrier and golden retriever.

12.   The breeds includes: spaniel, terrier and golden retriever.

13.   The cell phones in the display case is made in Korea.

14.   The cell phones in the display case are made in Korea.

15.   One of the presidents of Venezuela was ousted in January.

16.   One of the presidents of Venezuela were ousted in January.

Choose one of the words in parentheses to complete each of the sentences correctly.

17.   The expectations of the motivational speakers (is, are) unreasonably high.

18.   The nasty stain on the kitchen curtains (comes, come) from Princess Poltergeist drying her hands on them.

19.   Brantley's family roots (has, have) been traced back to the Garden of Eden.

20.   The forgotten rhinestone tiara in the basement (belongs, belong) to my cousin Batia.

21.   The size of frilly-petal Dutch tulips at Indiana Depot (is, are) enormous.

ANSWER KEY: SUBJECT/VERB AGREEMENT EXERCISE

The following sentences are correct. They have subjects and verbs that agree in person and number.

1.   *There were many B-movie stars in the rehearsal hall.*

3.   *The children in that family are adorable.*

6.   *Everybody usually watches the girls in Brazilian bikinis on the beach.*

7.   *Lorena* also *needs* to cut her sentences shorter.

9.   *He* is playing poker better because he *wants* to break the bank.

11.   The *breeds include*: spaniel, terrier and golden retriever.

14.   The cell *phones* in the display case *are* made in Korea.

15.   *One* of the presidents of Venezuela *was* ousted in January.

17.   The *expectations* of the motivational speakers (is, *are*) unreasonably high.

18.   The nasty *stain* on the kitchen curtains (*comes*, come) from Princess Poltergeist drying her hands on them.

19.   Brantley's family *roots* (has, *have*) been traced back to the Garden of Eden.

20.   The forgotten rhinestone *tiara* in the basement (*belongs*, belong) to my cousin Batia.

21.   The *size* of frilly-petal Dutch tulips at Indiana Depot (*is*, are) enormous.

Please write your journal entry for Chapter 12 **NOW**. For instructions, see Page 7.

YOUR NOTES HERE

CHAPTER 13: MINDING YOUR TONE

The faster you *read,* the more you *remember*. Audiences read sentences faster when those sentences sound more like normal speech than like something that escaped from a late 16ᵗʰ century bill of lading.

Overly formal speech will distance you from anyone who doesn't sound as formal as you do. The trouble with most "business" writing that comes across your desk every day is that it's too stiff. It makes the writer look stuffy, prissy, boring, or old-fashioned. Most writing can be streamlined by making your writing sound more like "talk."

The rule of thumb in finding the right tone in which to write someone is to write the way you'd actually talk to the reader if you were with him or her.

"Yo!" for example, may not be a proper way to address members of your Executive Board. Closing your e-mail request for IT information with "I remain your attentive and obedient servant," is not a good idea either.

In Chapter 13, we'll concentrate on :

- ♦ how to "talk" on paper.
- ♦ when to use contractions
- ♦ what form to use for private and business letters
- ♦ how to choose how many people to write to
- ♦ how to keep it interesting

If I had a $100 for everyone who tells me that: (a)"Transports of repository files are done upon proper user sign-off and management approval," sounds more "businesslike" than (b)"The audit department sends repository files after the user signs off; then management approves them," I wouldn't be teaching this course; I'd be having mint tea with Bedouins in Fez.

Look at sentence (a) for three seconds. Close your eyes and see if you can remember what it *means*. I don't mean what it says word for word, I mean what it *means*. Is the idea easy to remember? Could you tell someone else what the procedure was for transporting files if your pants were on fire?

Look at sentence (b) for three seconds. Close your eyes and see if you can remember what *it* means.

If the whole point of business writing is to get the reader to understand, remember and act on what you've written, which sentence is more "businesslike," sentence (a) or sentence (b)?

One difference between sentence (a) and sentence (b) is that (a) is written in the *passive* voice and (b) is written in the *active* voice. We spoke about passive and active voice in Chapter 5; here we'll expand on what we learned. We will also learn two fail-safe techniques for turning passives into actives.

Defining "voice"

When grammarians refer to "voice," they mean one of two things: the *active* voice (John threw the ball to Mary) or the *passive* voice (the ball was thrown to Mary by John). There are several differences between the two:

Passive Voice	Active Voice
Doesn't tell who's doing the action	**Tells who the "act-er" is**
Sounds stuffy	**Sounds alive**
Is difficult to understand	**Is easy to understand**
Is almost impossible to remember	**Is easy to remember**

Technically, the passive voice makes clear writing into what I call "upside-down writing." In speech, most sentences have a subject, a verb and an object (in that order). The passive voice turns things around and has an object, a verb and maybe, if you're lucky, a subject.

One way to spot a passive voice sentence when you see one, is to look for *who* did the action. If the act-er is missing you may have snagged an authentic passive voice sentence. Look through the papers that cross your desk this week and see how many passive sentences you can catch. **Do it NOW.**

> If you check the "Reading Statistics" box
> in your Grammar Check program, it will tell you
> the percentage of passive voice sentences
> you've used in any document you've written.

Having spotted some passive sentences and having gotten the feel for the difference between a lively active sentence and a dull clunky passive sentence in your own written work, you probably want to know how to solve the problem of passivity vs. activity quickly and easily.

There are two ways:

(1) **HUMAN IT UP:** Put human beings into the sentence. If you've got a human being, or a pronoun that stands for a human being doing the action, you've pretty much fixed the problem.

(2) **LUNCHROOM IT:** "Lunchrooming" means loosening and livening up a sentence by saying that sentence as you would say it to a friend over lunch. It will often get rid of the passive voice automatically because humans seldom speak in the passive voice.

Lunchrooming does three helpful things:

1. It makes your writing easy to "hear" and read.
2. It changes passive voice sentences into active voice sentences (most of the time)
3. It helps speed your readers' eyes through your document—saving them time and helping them remember what you've told them.

CONCEPT #48: *Lunchroom, lunchroom, lunchroom.*

Another tip-off that you've been writing in the passive voice is the overuse of the verb "to be" in any of its forms.

be	was	has been	will be
am	were	had been	would be
is			

These are the "to be" forms to look for. Let's look at the difference between a document written in the *passive* voice and one written in the *active* voice. This example comes from the marketing department of a large international bank:

PASSIVE VOICE

(1) *On November 28, approximately 3,000 letters will be mailed to certain potential customer segments. The letter has been designed to encourage the opening of money market accounts and has a mini-application form printed on the bottom. The customer is instructed to complete the application and return it in the enclosed business reply envelope to open an account. A sample copy of the letter has been attached for your reference. Each letter will be customized for each Branch Manager, and the quantity of letters mailed will vary for each branch.*

The writer uses some form of "to be" five times in five sentences.

ACTIVE VOICE

(2) *The Marketing Department is sending a mailing to a select group of potential customers who don't have money market accounts with us. We've designed the letter with a mini-application form at the bottom so people can open new accounts in your branch quickly and easily.*

148

We'll customize each letter for you, and we'll supply you with the number of letters appropriate for your branch. I've attached a copy of the letter for you to look at.

Which version do you like better (1) or (2)? Why?

Now analyze sentence (2) and find three concrete reasons it's different from sentence (1). **Do it NOW**.

1.

2.

3.

WANT TO IMPRESS THE BOSS? USE SMALL WORDS

A study from Stanford University concludes that people who use complicated language when simple words will do tend to be viewed as *less intelligent* than those who use a more basic vocabulary.

When people read simpler language, they actually rate the author's intelligence higher than they do the intelligence of those who write using large words and a more complex sentence structure. Don't use big words. Obfuscation hurts.

What big words do you use all the time? Write them here:

What can you replace them with?

Write these concepts (three to five times each) on a separate page:

Concept #49	Concept #50	Concept #51
Avoid $10 words.	Contractions are my friends.	I needn't tell everything to everyone.

BIG WORDS VS. SMALL WORDS

Most "how to write" books give you lists of words and phrases you can simplify. Sure you can memorize them, but, here's a little trick I learned from my friend Pascal: When you have a choice between a three-syllable word and a one-syllable word—choose the one-syllable word.

Why? Because one-syllable words are the oldest, strongest words in the English language. They pack the most punch. They deliver the goods the way longer words never can. Consider the difference between "reticule" and "bag." When was the last time any woman you know couldn't find her lipstick in her reticule?

Why use $10 words (like visage) when you can use nickel words (like face)? Would you pay $165 for a roaster/broiler when you knew you could get the same roaster/broiler on sale for $25? I rest my case.

CONCEPT #49: *Avoid multi-syllable $10 words.*

CONTRACTIONS

Not only is it *okay* to use contractions, it's *necessary*. Using contractions when you write makes what you're writing sound like everyday speech. Contractions are warm and friendly. They make the eye skip over the page quickly. You've probably noticed that I've used contractions all through these chapters. Would it have been quicker to read if I had written that last sentence like this: *"You have probably noticed that I have used contractions all through these chapters?"*

CONCEPT #50:   *Contractions are your friends.*

WHAT TO WRITE TO WHOM

Now that your writing is livelier, is it *effective*? Is it the right length to do the job? Is it too long for readers to get through it? Is it too short to get the job done?

When I was a child, my father told me that the proper length for any written piece of work was the same as the proper length for a mini-skirt:

"Short enough to be interesting, but long enough to cover the subject."

Let's call it "The Mini-skirt Rule."   How does this apply to people in business? Let's take the example of a participant in a seminar I gave not long ago. The man had two bosses. One was *very* technical and wanted to go over the minutest detail before approving anything. The other had the attention span of a gnat. What to do? How do you tell them *both* what they need to know in *one* memo?

The answer is, you *don't*. You write up the big picture and send it to your short-attention-spanned boss. Then you write up a detailed report for the other one. This takes much less time than trying to stuff all the information into one document. It increases the chances that both documents will get read. It also strengthens your relationships with both bosses by proving you care enough to talk to them intelligently.

CONCEPT #51:   *You needn't tell everything to everyone.*

Remember: the marketing director of Tacky Cosmetics will be most interested in seeing *sales figures* on the new Glow-in-the-Dark blusher promotion—the sales people will be most interested in *who* sold the most blusher and what company rewards they got for their efforts.

HEADLINES AND SUB-HEADS

Have you ever noticed how some people will immediately open the Sunday paper to the Sports Section while others grab for Arts and Leisure? People read what they're interested in. They skip over the other parts. So, if you're writing to people, it's best to try to give them only what interests them most. If you're writing to an audience of readers with different interests, *separate* the information into clearly marked parts. Open with a brief executive summary or an overview to satisfy the attention-span challenged, then attach a more extensive report for the detail buffs.

Separating information and clearly marking what that information contains is the reason your daily newspaper has headlines. The editors want you to skim through the pages and read what you're most interested in—first. People who write on the job use headlines and sub-heads for the same reason—to tell each reader where to find the important stuff. From the reader's point of view, of course.

CONCEPT #52: *If they're not reading, you're not writing.*

Please write your journal entry for Chapter 13 **NOW.** For instructions, see Page 7.

CHAPTER 14: PUNCTUATING PROPERLY?!

There's nothing mysterious about punctuation. Amazed? I shouldn't wonder. Most people writing for business cringe at the thought of punctuation. Some writers are comma-dependent, peppering everything they write with commas. Others leave the punctuation out altogether.

Either way, the result is hard to read and even harder to understand. Imagine talking to friends, telling them about what happened yesterday in the budget meeting. The story is alive and understandable because you gesture, make faces, drop or raise your voice and put long or short pauses in the appropriate places. But how do you get the same effect when you're not "live"?

Punctuation. That's right, periods and commas, dashes and dots. Used correctly, punctuation fills in for the color of spoken speech and puts your body language on paper. This Chapter will concentrate on simple guidelines for bringing your documents to life with punctuation. We'll talk about how to:

- ◆ demystify punctuation
- ◆ use a checklist
- ◆ practice punctuating correctly

I've never met anyone who is secure about his or her own knowledge of punctuation. In my experience, no one (who doesn't make a living teaching grammar) knows exactly where to put a comma, and where to leave one out. Personal research indicates that the semi-colon is more mysterious to most people than the Dead Sea Scrolls. Do periods go inside or outside quotation marks? When do you use parentheses? The insecurities are endless.

Luckily, many of the same questions about punctuation crop up repeatedly. I'll try to answer the most frequent questions, here. For more complete answers to your punctuation questions, and many other writing questions, you'll want to get a copy of : **The Business Writer's Handbook**, edited by Gerald Alred, Charles T. Brusaw and Walter E. Oliu. It's published by Bedford/St. Martin's and is available in a handy, spiral-bound paperback edition.

In addition to being an excellent resource for punctuation issues, this book is one of the best reference texts to have on the shelf. **The Business Writer's Handbook** has answers to, and examples of, almost anything you'll run into in your business-writing career.

How Important Is Punctuation, Anyway?

If you don't think punctuation matters, try reading the "copyright" paragraph (below) aloud, and see how you do with it.

(This explanation of copyright came to me as e-mail. I don't know who wrote it, but I'm very grateful it found its way to me.)

> copyright explained when you write copy you have the right to copyright the copy you write if the copy is right if however your copy falls over you must right your copy if you write religious services you write rite and have the right to copyright the rite you write very conservative people write right copy and have the right to copyright the right copy they write a right wing cleric would write right rite and has the right to copyright the right rite he has the right to write his editor has the job of making the right rite copy right before the copyright can be right should Jim Wright decide to write right rite then Wright would write right rite which Wright has the right to copyright duplicating that rite would copy Wright right rite and violate copyright which Wright would have the right to right right

Reading without punctuation wasn't easy; was it? Now, try reading the same paragraph punctuated correctly.

Copyright Explained

When you write copy you have the right to copyright the copy you write, if the copy is right. If however, your copy falls over, you must right your copy. If you write religious services, you write rite, and have the right to copyright the rite you write.

Very conservative people write right copy, and have the right to copyright the right copy they write. A right wing cleric would write right rite, and has the right to copyright the right rite he has the right to write. His editor has the job of making the right rite copy right before the copyright can be right.

Should Jim Wright decide to write right rite, then Wright would write right rite, which Wright has the right to copyright. Duplicating that rite would copy Wright right rite, and violate copyright, which Wright would have the right to right. Right?

PUNCTUATION AND TONE

When people talk with each other they make themselves understood by using body language (gestures, facial expressions) tone of voice (questioning, emphatic, whiny, sad) and other cues (such as pauses) that can't be written down. Here's an example of how tone of voice can change when you change the punctuation:

DIRECTIONS: Read letters A and B. They are identical except for their punctuation.

Letter A

Dear John,

    I want a man who knows what love is all about. You are generous, kind, thoughtful. People who are not like you admit to being useless and inferior. You have ruined me for other men. I yearn for you. I have no feelings whatsoever when we're apart. I can be forever happy—will you let me be yours?

    Gloria

Turn the page now to see Letter B.

Letter B

Dear John,

I want a man who knows what love is. All about you are generous, kind, thoughtful people, who are not like you. Admit to being useless and inferior. You have ruined me. For other men, I yearn. For you, I have no feelings whatsoever. When we're apart, I can be forever happy. Will you let me be?

Yours,

Gloria

Please write (in the space below) why correct punctuation is important.

Ideally, punctuation should be invisible to your readers—they shouldn't be *aware* of your punctuation, they should just be able to follow the story and make heads or tails out of it.

Most writers know the basics:

- Use a period at the end of a sentence. *The calla lilies are in bloom again.*
- Use a question mark at the end of a question. *What do you think he meant?*
- Use an exclamation point at the end of an exclamation. *Ouch! That hurts!*

Note: There is seldom a real reason for using exclamation points in business writing. Use them sparingly because they make you sound childishly over-enthusiastic!!!

Sounds simple enough, so why does punctuation scare people? Probably because they assume there are hundreds of punctuation marks, and that nobody ever mentioned how to use them correctly. The bad news is that there *are* 30 main punctuation marks. The good news is that most of us need less than a dozen to get by. Most people I've met seem to have four major punctuation issues they'd like to deal with:

- how to use commas correctly
- what semicolons are and where to use them
- where to put a colon and what to do after you put it there
- when to use a period, when not to

Let's take those issues one by one.

COMMAS

There are people who recommend using commas every time you'd take a short pause if you were speaking. That's fine, but some people pause more than others and some people don't pause at all.

The problem with throwing commas in whenever you'd pause is, if you use them incorrectly, they can change the meaning of your sentence. Completely.

Look at these two sentences,

a. *The staff, says the boss, is incompetent.*

b. *The staff says the boss is incompetent.*

Which one means that the staff doesn't think much of the boss' ability to do his job? Right. Sentence *b*.

Without commas, or with commas in the wrong places, it's difficult to tell what a writer means. I'm going to make it easy, though.

1. Use a comma after lengthy introductory material:

    While interviewing an executive assistant over a chilled Red Zinger, I filed my nails.

Note: Don't use a comma after *brief* introductory material:

    After interviewing the assistant I went home for a chilled Red Zinger.

2. To separate items in a series:

    I interviewed the assistant, drank a chilled Red Zinger, called Antonio, read the mail *and filed my nails.

*I didn't use a comma before the final "and" in this series because I'm trying to be modern. Anyone who went to grade school after 1975 leaves that final comma out.

Here's another example of items in a series:

    His itinerary includes trips to Boston, Beijing, Kuala Lumpur and Barcelona.

Here's an un-punctuated example of items in a series:

    The farmer raised sheep dogs and turkeys.

Do you know how many kinds of livestock the farmer raised? Some people say three: sheep, dogs and turkeys. Some say two: sheep dogs and turkeys. How many critters did you think the farmer raised?

3. We use commas to rope off wedged-in ideas that aren't essential to the sentence.

   *Red Zingers, **which have always interested me**, are best when they're cold.*

4. To separate two complete clauses that are joined by a linking word like ***and, but, for, or, because,*** or ***so***:

   *I shall hire the assistant, **because** he is so handsome.*

5. To directly address someone:

   *I'm not kidding, **Harold**, be serious.*

6. To separate names from their titles:

   *Drusilla Lovelace, **Attorney General**, appeared for the prosecution.*

7. To separate elements of a geographical address:

   *Ms. Lovelace was born in **Bilbao, Spain** and now lives in Moosejaw, Canada.*

Do we need a comma before the "and" in example seven? That's a matter of contention. The *old garde* says "yes" while modern writers and editors, who are moving toward fewer and fewer commas, say "no." You can take your pick, but either way you choose—be consistent. Bouncing around from one style to another clutters the page and confuses the readers.

PARENTHESES ( )

Like commas, parentheses also mark off "wedged-in" information. The problem with parentheses is that whatever's inside them sounds like a whispered aside:

Brenda (who, between you and me is a complete idiot) is coming to the party.

Parenthetical information can be annoying if overused, because it sounds like nine-year-old girls sharing secrets in the schoolyard.

SEMICOLONS (;)

The semicolon is the comma's sophisticated older sister. It separates two complete sentences while joining their ideas closer together than periods do. For example:

She's a bimbo; he's a geek.

Use semicolons when you want to link ideas or break up a patch of short, choppy sentences.

COLONS (:)

Colons announce things. They separate them from the main part of the sentence–and say them in a loud voice. For example:

Men only want one thing: toys.

You'll also notice a colon after the salutation in formal letters:

Dear Ms. Earwax:

(If you're writing an *informal* letter, use a comma after your salutation: *Dear Ophelia,)*

Colons also introduce a list:

Groceries: eye of newt, hair of bat, goat milk, brown sugar, fertilized eggs, clarified butter

APOSTROPHES (')

Apostrophes show possession:

John's petri dish.

If the owners of the thing you're talking about have a last name that ends with "s," the apostrophe goes after the final "s."

The Jones' velociraptor.

If you have a singular noun ("Esme," "troglodyte," "intern") add ('s) to it to make it possessive.

Esme's garter belt.

If your noun is plural ("cannibals," "teen-agers," "dolts") add an apostrophe after the s:

These are the cannibals' omelet pans.

"Its" is a word that shows possession but *doesn't* take an apostrophe at all.

The university gets angry if you rough up its professors.

If you throw an apostrophe between the "t" and the "s" what you've written is the contraction for "it is":

It's a lovely day today. It's so nice I think I'll give the cat its caviar.

HYPHENS (-)

Hyphens connect two adjectives that, when linked together, make one idea.

"It's a 50 karat, blue-white, gem-quality diamond."

"He's a six-year-old Schnauzer."

Hyphens are also used to separate a word be-tween syllables at the end of a line.

QUOTATION MARKS

Quotation marks enclose the exact words someone says: *"It stinks," she said.* Or , *Hepsebah said, "It stinks."* Notice that the comma comes inside the quotation marks in the first example, but before them in the second. Don't ask why.

Don't use quotation marks when you're reporting what someone said: *She said it stank.*

ELLIPSES (...)

Otherwise known as "dot, dot, dot," ellipses stand for something that is left out. Say you've quoted a piece of Hamlet's speech to the players (as I do below) but haven't used the entire speech. The ellipsis shows there was extra material you didn't use.

1)   *"Speak the speech I pray you, as I pronounced it to you, trippingly on the tongue..."*

Use an ellipsis at the beginning of a quote to show that there is material left out before the material you're using.

"...I had as lief the Town Crier spoke my lines."

If you've ever seen an ad for a new play, you'll realize that producers use ellipses to cut out pesky negative text that falls in between kudos in reviews. The billboard in front of the theater may read:

"Passionate...brilliant..."

The original review may have read:

*"The **passionate** performances of the cast could not make up for the weak plot. **Brilliant** it wasn't."*

PUNCTUATION RECAP

periods	signal the end of statements	*I think I'm late.*
question marks	signal the end of questions.	*Is the queen mother tipsy again?*
hyphens 1:	separate syllables at the ends of lines	*Burt never does his home-work.*
hyphens 2:	connect two words that form one thought	*Henry insists on having world-class toys.*
dashes:	create a billboard for information that follows	*His voice was—divine.*
	insert a dramatic pause	
commas 1:	separate introductory material from the main clause.	*Because her high heels were broken, she was late for the matinee.*
		If you're mad, you ought to see the witchdoctor.

commas 2:	mark off "wedged-in" ideas when the commas are used in pairs.	*Members of the audience who didn't like Heavy Metal music, left the concert hall.*
commas 3:	signal that you're talking directly to someone	*"Don't eat, Henry, before your father comes downstairs."*
commas 4:	separate items in a series of three or more	*She wanted to marry Curly, Moe, Larry and Marvin.*
		Senator Bernhardt promised to lower taxes, solve the economic problem, end unemployment, increase Social Security and put a chicken in every pot.
commas 5:	introduce direct quotes	*Lucille said, "You're a foolish cow."*
	set off direct quotes from the rest of the sentence	*"You're a foolish cow," said Lucille.*
commas 6:	set off geographical names	*Pittsburgh, PA*
	items in dates	*June 3, 2025*
	addresses	*1600 Caballeros Drive, Palm Springs, CA*
	titles	*Yehuda Shandling, Ph.D.,*

commas 7:	end informal salutations	*Dear Raymond,*
semicolons:	separate two complete sentences	*I was brought into this world on Thursday, March 28, 1833; my eyes did not see daylight, but rather that of a tallow candle.*
	link two complete sentences together more closely than periods	
colons 1:	announce the start of a list	*Wilson's itinerary includes: Uberlandia, Uberaba, and Ubatuba.*
colons 2:	end a formal salutation	*Dear Dr. Stillskin:*
exclamation points:	follow words or sentences written with emotion	*Ouch! Oh, my word! I collided with a man dressed like Mr. Peanut!*
apostrophes:	mark possession	*It's Carly's book. They're Morticia Adams' portraits.*
quotation marks:	enclose direct speech	*"Phooey," he said.*
parentheses:	enclose wedged-in (or explanatory) information	*Martha (a certified witch) produced a line of sheets and towels.*

PUNCTUATION EXERCISE #1

The sentences below can mean completely different things depending on the way they are punctuated. The punctuation involved may be a comma, or commas, a semicolon, an apostrophe, a hyphen, a question mark, or a period. Or, the sentence may not need punctuation.

DIRECTIONS: See if you can punctuate each sentence so that it matches the description that follows it.

1. The damsel wanted to know if she should stick the stamp on herself. (She'll need lots of postage)

   The damsel wanted to know if she should stick the stamp on herself. (She'll need normal postage)

2. The Cabinet says the King is incompetent. (The King criticizes the Cabinet)

   The Cabinet says the King is incompetent. (The King won't be happy to hear this)

3. Seventeen choirboys knew professor Munchkin's secret all told. (There were 17 altogether.)

   Seventeen choirboys knew Professor Munchkin's secret all told. (The choirboys were not loyal)

4. Mr. Knight the alchemist is two hours late.
    (The alchemist, Blanche Marker, is about to be scolded)

    Mr. Knight the alchemist is two hours late.
    (Mr. Knight is about to be scolded)

5. Go slow children. (A warning to children)

    Go slow children. (A warning to drivers)

6. Countess Glaznarovna asked the footman to call the guests names as they
    arrived. (Embarrassing)

    Countess Glaznarovna asked the footman to call the guests names as they
    arrived. (Appropriate)

ANSWER KEY: PUNCTUATION EXERCISE #1

1. *The damsel wanted to know if she should stick the stamp on herself. (She'll need lots of postage)*

    The damsel wanted to know if she should stick the stamp on, herself. (She'll need normal postage)

2. *The Cabinet, says the King, is incompetent. (The King criticizes the Cabinet)*

    The Cabinet says the King is incompetent. (The King won't be happy to hear this)

3. *Seventeen choirboys knew professor Munchkin's secret, all told. (There were 17 altogether.)*

    Seventeen choirboys knew Professor Munchkin's secret, all told. (The choirboys were not loyal)

4.   *Mr. Knight, the alchemist is two hours late. (The alchemist, Blanche Marker, is about to be scolded)*

   Mr. Knight, the alchemist, is two hours late. (Mr. Knight is about to be scolded)

5.   *Go slow, children. (A warning to children)*

   Go slow, children. (A warning to drivers)

6.   *Countess Glaznarovna asked the footman to call the guests names as they arrived. (Embarrassing)*

   Countess Glaznarovna asked the footman to call the guests' names as they arrived. (Appropriate)

PUNCTUATION EXERCISE #2

DIRECTIONS: Please put apostrophes (and letters) wherever they're needed. Remove the apostrophes where they're not.

1.   Both manager month-long vacations caused a delay in launching the new lipsticks.

2.   I went to my mother-in-law house to make enraged phone calls to Senators.

3.   It's beauty is unremarkable.

4.   The monk pocket was full of tiny diamonds.

5.   The cantor coming was completely unexpected. (one cantor)

6.   Most stockbrokers children imaginations run wild when you tell them the Enron story.

7.   Its hard to believe we've won the lottery.

8.   The pelican vitality and humor were infectious. (one pelican)

9.   The poison had it's way with the Prime Minister.

10.   The women dresses are on the balcony.

11.   You can't go into the princess bedroom without the prince permission.

12.   You're right to a fair trial will not be acknowledged.

13.   Its a miracle!

ANSWER KEY: PUNCTUATION EXERCISE #2

1.   Both managers' month-long vacations caused a delay in launching the new lipsticks.

2.   I went to my mother-in-law's house to make enraged phone calls to Senators.

3.   Its beauty is unremarkable.

4.   The monk's pocket was full of tiny diamonds.

5.   The cantor's coming was completely unexpected.

6.   Most stockbrokers' children's imaginations run wild when you tell them the Enron story.

7.   It's hard to believe we've won the lottery.

8.   The pelican's vitality and humor were infectious.

9.   The poison had its way with the Prime Minister.

10.   The women's dresses are on the balcony.

11.   You can't go into the princess' bedroom without the prince's permission.

12.   Your right to a fair trial will not be acknowledged.

13.   It's a miracle!

By this time, you should feel a bit more secure about using punctuation to get your thoughts on paper.

Here are some websites where you can test yourself.

PUNCTUATION WEBSITES

http://owl.english.purdue.edu/handouts/grammar/
http://webster.commnet.edu/grammar/quiz_list.htm
http://www.grammarbook.com/
http://www.brownlee.org/durk/grammar/quizpage.html

Important: Punctuation is not something you can expect Grammar Check to help you with. It's only software and easily confuses statements with questions, so trust your brain and your ear and your checklist.

Write these concepts (three to five times each) on a separate page:

Concept #55	Concept #56	Concept #57
Beware of certainty.	Don't guess; check.	Double-check even if I'm sure it's right.

Please write your journal entry for Chapter 14 **NOW.** For instructions, see Page 7.

CHAPTER 15: FORMATTING FOR HUMAN BEINGS

I keep saying: "The faster we read the more we remember." I touched on it in terms of organization, grammar, and sentence structure. But, even if you have all those things in place and your organization, grammar, and sentence structure are picture perfect, your writing may be impossible to read.

Surprised? In this Chapter we'll examine *how* people read and how formatting, white space, headlines and bullet points can help readers remember what they read more easily.

THE "OH NO! DO I HAVE TO READ THIS?" FORMAT

The memo you're about to read came over the Internet several years ago. I have just one question for you: How do you *feel* about reading it?

MEMO

TO: Cyril R. Huffnickle
FROM: Guy Wired

DATE: November 19, 2044
RE: Poultry Project

Deregulation of the chicken's side of the road was threatening its dominant market position. The chicken was faced with significant challenges to create and develop the competencies required for the newly competitive market. A-Z Consulting, in a partnering relationship with the client, helped the chicken by rethinking its physical distribution strategy and implementation processes. Using the Poultry Integration Model (PIM), A-Z helped the chicken use its skills, methodologies, knowledge, capital and experiences to align the chicken's people processes and technology in support of its overall strategy within a Program Management framework. A-Z Consulting convened a diverse cross-spectrum of road analysts and best chickens along with A-Z consultants with deep skills in the transportation industry to engage in a two-day itinerary of meetings in order to leverage their personal knowledge capital, both tacit and explicit, and to enable them to synergize with each other in order to achieve the implicit goals of delivering and successfully architecting and implementing an enterprise-wide value framework across the continuum of poultry cross-median processes. The meeting was held in a park-like setting, enabling and creating an impactful environment which was strategically based, industry-focused, and built upon a consistent, clear and unified market message and aligned with the chicken's mission, vision, and core values. This was conducive towards the creation of a total business integration solution. A-Z Consulting helped the chicken change to become more successful.

Frightening, isn't it? Forget the content or the amazing amount of $10 words and passive voice constructions. Think about your *physical* reaction. Your body recoils just to look at such a dense block of type. It's intimidating. Your eyes don't want to make the effort. Your stomach churns. Especially if you have to read it *carefully*, or if you have to mine it for vital information. Your head aches. You need a cup of cocoa. You stick the memo at the bottom of your in-box and hope it will go away.

When you finally get around to reading the memo, you stop and start. You constantly go back to the beginning of the sentence to find out what's going on with the chicken and A-Z's strategies. You read and re-read.

Imagine how much of your time is wasted reading and re-reading badly formatted documents because you didn't understand them the first time around. Imagine all the things you would be doing if you saved all this wasted time and got out of the office at 5:00 P.M. instead of 8:00. Imagine how valuable you might be to your company bigwigs if you showed them how much money they could save by spiffing up some writing skills.

We live in a culture with an MTV attention span. The last thing we want to do is sit down with a big dense block of copy written in a mouse-poop size font. It's off-putting. So, what's the answer?

WHITE SPACE

White space looks friendly. This book is written in brief paragraphs surrounded by white space because brief chunks of material make reading seem like less work. Writing, *good* writing, takes a good ear, so your documents look and sound like a conversation with plenty of spaces for the reader to step in and ask questions. Or think. Or slip off to the fridge to get another Diet Pepsi.

GENEROUS BORDERS

Not only do generous borders give your document enough space to breathe, they contain the information you're trying to convey so your readers don't feel assaulted by it. Generous borders are like the difference between listening to a well-thought out presentation and listening to someone who babbles on…and on…and on…and on…and on…and on.

There are two points to remember about good formatting. One is to make it easier for readers to find information they need. The second is to help readers' eyes move quickly from the top to the bottom of the page. *"Quickly"* is the key word here. Because (once again) the faster you read, the more you remember—so anything that interrupts your forward motion (a) annoys you and (b) makes you more liable to forget, or trash, what you're reading.

HEADLINES

Reading a document without headlines is taking a cross-country trip without a map. The best way to drive from New York City to Kennebunkport is to follow the signs. If there were no signs it would be much more difficult to find your way and you'd waste a lot of time wandering around in southern Maine lost and frustrated. Such is the position of a reader expected to read a long document without the benefit of headlines.

Headlines, titles and sub-heads make it easier to scan down a document and concentrate on things that are important to you. Think of the way you read a magazine. You don't start at the masthead and read every word of every article straight through to the last page, do you? You turn to the headlines (*The Truth about Seabiscuit; 75 Things to do in Bed without Getting Arrested; New Study Proves FOOD is Harmful to Your Health*) and go straight to the article that interests you most. A good headline helps you through a business document because it tells you what's in the paragraphs below it. Then it leaves the choice up to you. If you're primarily concerned with the technical aspects of the new computer system, you might go directly to the headline that says: *"50-50 Push-Pull Components."* If you're more concerned with who's going to be responsible for keeping the new computer system up and running, you'd go to *"Installation and Maintenance."*

BULLETS

Bullets make information easier to find. If you have the choice, dig information out of the paragraph and put it in bullet form. One thing to remember about bullets is the importance of *parallel structure*. Put all your bullet points in the same form. If you start the first bullet with a verb, all the following bullets need to start with a verb. If you start with a noun, *all* the bullets need to start with a noun.

VERBS	NOUNS
Be concise	*Interviews* with mermaids
Start swiftly	*Invitations* to consultants
Write clearly	*Reports* on sea-monkeys
End positively	*Expenses* re Transylvania trip

AN AUTHENTIC EXAMPLE OF BAD BULLETS

This bulleted list comes from a class called: "The Art of Public Speaking." Read the following bulleted list out loud. Can you *hear* what's wrong with it? Can you *feel* what's wrong with it?

What You Can Expect from this Class

- Powerful Coaching
- Feedback from the Group
- Opportunity to Evaluate Others
- Make a Presentation
- Learn by Doing
- To Focus Your Strengths
- To Work on Your Weaknesses
- Gain Valuable Experiences

Right. What's wrong with this list is its lack of rhythm, its stop-and-go motion, its jumbled thought pattern. See if you can fix the list to make it parallel. **Do it NOW.**

FONT

When I taught a course in Dusseldorf, the participants all complained about the font I was using. I liked it because it looked like hand printing and I thought it was friendly but distinctive. Unfortunately, as friendly and distinctive as I thought it was, it was almost impossible for the people taking the workshop to read. The first thing I did when I got back to the U. S. was change all my materials to a more readable font.

What makes a font *readable*? Serifs. Serifs are the little curves or "flat tails" that appear at the upper and lower ends of some fonts. **Palatino Linotype** is a serif font. This book is written in Palatino Linotype. **Arial** is a *sans* serif font. Note Arial's missing little tails?

Look back at Guy Wired's memo to Cyril R. Huffnickle (the chicken memo). It's written in Arial (a sans serif font). Coupled with everything else that's wrong with Guy Wired's memo, the lack of serifs stop the eyes' movement for an instant at every letter. Fonts with serifs make reading easier because your eyes move swiftly along their curves. The more swiftly your eyes move, the faster you read. Think of a roller coaster versus stop-and-go traffic.

There *is* one font designed specifically to be easy to read on PC screen. It's called Verdana. Use it liberally for documents that won't end up as hard copy. This paragraph is written in Verdana.

You've heard of handwriting analysis. Well, I'm going to propose an art called "document formatting analysis." Here are the things to look for and what each of them (according to my extremely personal system) means:

DOCUMENT FORMATTING ANALYSIS

MARGINS	wide	writer is generous
	narrow	writer is stingy, lacks consideration or reserve, has limited paper supply
SPACE AT TOP	wide	writer has respect for person being written to
	narrow	writer is indifferent to his/her audience.
SPACE AT BOTTOM	wide	writer is aloof or reserved
	narrow	writer is materialistic, may be depressed, can't bear to use a new page
TYPE SIZE	11 point	writer is honest cares about reader's eyesight
	mouse type (8 point)	writer may be hiding something in the fine print
		writer's company is not doing well and needs to save paper

PARAGRAPH SIZE	relatively short	writer has thought his subject through carefully and is giving readers the information in easy-to-digest pieces
	very long	writer may be confused or may be filling the page with excess blah-blah. Writer isn't sure where one idea stops and another begins.
FONT SIZE	large	writer is extroverted and wants to make a big impression on the world.
	small	writer is modest or is presenting a modest proposal, or doesn't want the reader to read the fine print all that carefully.

E-MAIL

E-mail has its own rules. Not surprisingly, I have some prejudices about them. For example, I loathe "emoticons" — ☹. I think adults should be able to express themselves clearly and honestly in words. I think by the time you're fourteen you should know that sarcasm seldom works in print, and that if a thought is truly funny you don't need a smiley face to drive the point home ☺.

IT'S UNWISE TO PUT A SHOCKING BACKGROUND COLOR BEHIND YOUR E-MAIL MESSAGES BECAUSE YOUR READER HAS TO SQUINT TO READ WHAT YOU'RE SAYING.

UNUSUALLY LARGE FONT SIZES RESEMBLE CLUMPS OF CAPITAL LETTERS. THE READER SUBCONSCIOUSLY BACKS AWAY FROM THE MESSAGE BECAUSE HUGE FONTS LOOK LIKE THE WRITER IS YELLING.

BOILERPLATE

Boilerplate is handy, but dangerous. "Boilerplate" is that word, sentence or paragraph you automatically put into letters, proposals and contracts. *"In order to create training materials, you must meet the following basic technical requirements"* is boilerplate. So is *"We'll keep your résumé on file and contact you if the situation changes."* You use the boilerplate phrase, sentence or paragraph so often, that in most cases, you can hit one key and the whole thing will appear like magic on the page. This is a great advantage of working with macros on a PC. It's also one of its greatest pitfalls.

Let me tell you about a proposal I sent to a prospective client. The man was President of a large Japanese mining company. Let's call him, "Mr. Okamoto." The proposal I sent him was fine until he got to the second page where I carefully explained the way we'd work together and suddenly his name disappeared and the names. "Mr. and Mrs. Marc H. Puppybreath" appeared in its place. It was boilerplate. I'd inserted it when I was in a hurry. I forgot there was a name mentioned that had to be changed. I also forgot that the pronouns (him) and (her) (them) would have to be changed. Net-net, I looked like an idiot and lost the job. There's nothing like a big mistake to teach a lesson. This mistake, especially since it hit me in the pocketbook, was my boilerplate college education.

Another thing to consider when you're using boilerplate is whether the tone of the boilerplate matches the tone of *your* part of the document. It's like hitting a psychological wind shear to go from *"The lunch was delightful. It was super to see you again and I'm really looking forward to starting our project..."* to *"This letter will confirm our pricing structure for private consultation..."* So, whenever you use boilerplate, be particularly vigilant and check everything *before* the boilerplate and everything *after* to see that you don't look schizophrenic.

Please write your journal entry for Chapter 15 **NOW.** For instructions, see Page 7.

YOUR NOTES HERE

CHAPTER 16: POOFREADING CAREFULY

Hardly anyone proofreads any more. E-mail is full of errors. Memos and letters abound with typos. Even contracts are riddled with mistakes. Nobody likes to proofread. Who has time? Besides, once I've written something, it's much harder to see typos and mistakes because my eyes and mind see what I *meant* to write rather than what I actually *wrote*.

This Chapter presents three timesaving ways to proofread that *won't* have you tearing your hair and *will* increase the likelihood of your being able to sign your name to your document confidently. In this Chapter, we'll:

- ♦ demonstrate why proofreading is worth the effort
- ♦ practice proofreading
- ♦ examine actual documents that haven't been proofread.

Think proofreading isn't important? I knew a food writer who neglected to proofread a recipe and ended up with a lethal ingredient in her Five-Alarm Texas-style Chili. Luckily, her editor caught the error before it went to print.

One of my favorite proofreading mishap stories, although I'm told it's apocryphal, is the one about Dr. Ruth Westheimer, author of "Sex for Dummies" who cautioned (in one of her earlier books) that sexually active teens should not use protection. If you read that last sentence carefully, you can identify with Dr. Ruth's reaction when she found that the erroneous *not* had slipped through the proofreading process, appearing in who knows how many hundreds of thousands of books that then had to be recalled.

Be careful. Sloppy proofreading *can* cause pregnancy.

Once you've written, revised, and edited, the one thing that can make the difference between being accepted as a credible professional and being seen as an idiot, is proofreading.

Let me tell you a tale. I had some knee problems and went to physical therapy for about three months, three times a week. At the end of my course of therapy, I got the following letter from the Physical Therapy institute. It wasn't a complicated letter, but this is how it read:

> Please sign the in close document and returned to
> "FisEd" at your earliest convenience.

Now this is a place that lists the Managing Editor of the NBC Nightly News, the ABC News President, and the Executive Editor of The Met Golfer on its advisory board. Imagine how embarrassed they'd be to see what was going out on their letterhead.

I am a terrible proofreader. I'm pathetic. There is at least one typo (typographical error) in everything I write. This book was full of typos. Just how full came to light only after a professional proofreader had a go at it.

Sometimes I catch mistakes before I mail something off to a client. Sometimes I don't catch them until months later when I'm reading over what I've written. Sometimes I just ruin an event in the here and now.

To prove exactly how weak I am at proofreading and how much havoc ensued because of my negligence—if you look at page 183 you'll find a copy of an invitation letter I sent to thirty friends and relatives. Read it carefully because the problem with it isn't obvious. If you think you've figured out what's wrong, write your guess in the space below.

Dear Friend,

I'm writing to invite you to a special event: The Graduation of my Presentation Skills Class at East Earmuff University.

Our graduation class will be held:

>Monday evening
>April 22, 2002
>From 6:15 to 8:20 P.M.
>East Earmuff's School of Continuing and Professional Studies
>203 East 15th Street (between Second and Third Avenues)
>Room 403

Judging from the presentations we've seen so far, graduation promises to be an extremely interesting evening.

I'd love you to be there.

Please e-mail me to let me know if you'll be joining us.

Thanks,

K. T. Maclay

Lots of people e-mailed me to say they were coming but only four people showed up. Why? What was the proofing error? Can you find it? Of course not, because it doesn't look like a typo or a misspelling. It's in the address: 203 East 15th Street is actually between Second and *First* Avenues, not Second and Third. And that's why, even though many confused invitees were wandering around on 15th Street between Second and Third Avenues, no one showed up. I'd given them the wrong address because I hadn't proofread the letter carefully enough.

CONCEPT #53: *Errors wreck credibility.*

Write these concepts (three to five times each) on a separate page:

Concept #52	Concept #53	Concept #54
If *they're* not reading, *I'm* not writing.	Errors wreck credibility.	Focus is my friend.

There are several problems with proofreading for typos. It's a bore. It's picky. It's time consuming. If you have 30 other things on your desk, do you really want to spend time reading everything over carefully?

The big problem with proofing your own work is that your *eyes* automatically correct errors. An *e* becomes an *o*. A semicolon looks like a colon. The word *"your"* becomes *"you're."* Spell check will not highlight any word that exists in the real world, so if you've written *"you're"* instead of *"your,"* or "too" instead of "to" or "forum" instead of "form," you're on your own. Spell check won't help you.

Careful writers have worked out systems that make proofing somewhat easier, and we'll look at them point by point:

PRINT IT OUT, THEN READ IT

Catching errors is easier when you're looking at hard copy. It's also easier to "blue pencil" (proofread and correct) hard copy at lunch, or while you're off the California coast fishing for marlin.

Note: Grammar check just told me: "**... while you're off the California coast fishing for marlin,**" was *incorrect* and should be written as: "**...while you *is* off the California coast fishing for marlin.**" This is why trusting your grammar check program to catch and fix your errors is folly.

READ OUT LOUD

Your *ears* will catch things your *eyes* don't see. Reading aloud is especially handy for catching extra words, repeated words or words you've accidentally left out. Reading aloud is also convenient because you can do it by yourself. You can even read aloud on a crowded bus or airplane. People will not think you're crazy. They'll think you're on your cell phone.

There is software called ViaVoice (from IBM) that will actually *read* your document to you out loud. The program is inexpensive and worth its weight in proofreading time saved.

READ YOUR DOCUMENT OUT LOUD *TO SOMEONE ELSE*

Let the other person read the final copy while you read from the original, corrected version. Try to find someone who's not involved in the project you're working on and has no particular interest in what you're writing about. A fresh pair of eyes will catch mistakes you never will.

LET THE DOCUMENT COOL

Write at the end of the day. Put what you've written in a drawer. Go to a ball game, play hockey, take a friend to the movies. Get a good night's sleep, then edit first thing in the morning. Most of us don't have time to let work sit overnight, but even if writing cools for a hour or two it'll look fresher when you pick it up again to proof it.

READ IT BACKWARDS, ONE WORD AT A TIME

Our eyes take in a word or phrase in less than half a second. We look at the general shape of a word and take it in as a whole. In ordinary reading, we automatically fill in the blanks. We read *"stragedy"* for *"strategy," "lose"* for *"loose"* and *"horseradish"* for *"heresiarch."* (A *heresiarch* is the founder or chief of a sect of heretics, in case you were wondering.)

Reading backwards prevents you from misinterpreting words. Helps keep you from filling in the blanks with what you *think* (logically) should be on the page. You know for certain the word *"horseradish"* doesn't belong in your quarterly report on Mexican politics, so seeing *"horseradish"* in black-and-white sends up a red flag for you to look more closely at the *"horseradish"* sentence. Reading backwards can pick up spelling glitches, extra words or dropped punctuation.

CHECK THE MATH, THEN CHECK IT AGAIN

Anytime you use a number, percentage, or fraction—that number, percentage, or fraction needs proofing. Here are some number things to look for:

♦ Make sure the number of steps in a list is the same number of steps you've promised in your text

♦ Double check the items in a numbered list to make sure that the numbers run concurrently, that no number is repeated and no number is left out

♦ Make sure you have a correct sum at the end of a column of figures

♦ If you mention percentages of a whole, be certain that your total adds up to 100%

> Use a blank sheet of paper
> to cover the material
> you haven't proofed yet.

Looking at a page with a lot of print on it tempts your eyes to move around. Covering up the text to come lets you concentrate on one line at a time.

CONCEPT #54: *Focus is your friend*

> Keep a list of your most frequent errors
> watch out for them when you proof

I'm constantly fighting a battle between "your" and "you're." My fingers type one when I'm thinking another. "To" and "too" are problem words. "Its" and "It's" bother me. I know I'm prone to make these mistakes repeatedly, so I'm always on the alert for them when I proofread.

CHECK ALL PROPER NAMES TWICE

Does Bloomingdale's have an apostrophe? Does Macy's ?

Concentrate on little words like "or," "of," "it," and "is." Little words are often interchanged.

CONCEPT #55: *Beware of certainty*

PROOFREADING CHECKLIST

Unmatched Boilerplate	Make sure it matches the tone of the rest of the document.
Inaccurate Spacing	Are there extra spaces between words? Are there enough spaces between paragraphs?

Extra/Missing Punctuation

Have you used an extra comma? Have you left out a comma? Does your punctuation make your writing more difficult to understand, or does it make your writing easier?

Extra Letters

Have you spelled kisss with three *s's*?

Missing Letters

Hve you dropped a vowel?

Extra Words

Have you repeated a word unintentionally? "They send their work to her she; she sends the specific comments back to them."

Missing Words

Have you written: "We believe that seminar has served its purpose," instead of "We believe that *the* seminar has served its purpose"?

Incorrect Honorifics

Are you sure the man's name is Mr. Bahary? Or should he be addressed as Dr. Bahary? Should your letter be addressed to Dr. and Mrs. Bahary, or to Dr. William Bahary and Countess Cilly Glasnorovna? Is it *Mr.* K. T. Maclay or *Ms.* K. T. Maclay or *Mrs.* Otis Hardy Maclay II? Check that you've used the right title (honorific) before sending the document to people. The wrong name will tick people off.

Errant Capital Letters

Is the season that follows winter spelled *Spring*? Or is it spelled *spring*? Is *president* spelled with a capital "p" when it's not being used in direct address?

Incomplete Sets of " " or ( )	Did you start a "quote but forget to stop it? Have you both started (and ended your parenthetical asides?
Incorrect State Name Abbreviations	Is Pennsylvania abbreviated PA or Penn.?
Misspelled Words	Have you mispelled anything? Look it up.
Missing Hyphenation	Is double-checked one word or two words with a hyphen between them?
Ie and ei Mix-Ups	Is it "chief" or "cheif," "recieve" or "receive?"
Mistyped Numbers	Have you confused your readers by putting page 31 between page 12 and page 14? Are your page numbers consecutive between chapters, or does Chapter 2 end with page 27 and Chapter Three begin with page 27?

CONCEPT #56: *Don't guess; check*

Here's some warm-up proofing practice. Each of the four texts on the next page has a mistake that gives a word an extra letter. If the word should be *"love,"* it's printed as *"glove."* As in *"Dear Helen, the entire third regiment sends you lots and lots of glove."* See if you can find the errors in these short pieces. **Do it NOW.**

```
HOTEL PARADISE

◆  186 comfortable rooms
◆  all with TV and telephone
◆  good views of the seat
◆  2 restaurants
◆  15 minutes from airport
◆  reasonable rates
```

General Gizmo, New Jersey's gift to the U.S. infantry, lost his army in a disturbing car crash last week.

```
PHONE INSTRUCTIONS

1.  Lift receiver

2.  Insert monkey

3.  Dial number and wait for connection

4.  Replace receiver when finished speaking.
```

NEW YORK CITY, July 15, 2001—Fifteen people became ill after drinking the waiter at a City Center restaurant yesterday. Composer Jane-Ellen Blaithewhistle was taken outside to get some fresh hair after collapsing at the bar.

CONCEPT #57:   *Double-check even if you're sure it's right.*

PROOFREADERS' MARKS

There is a set of symbols called "proofreaders' marks" that can help eliminate illegible chicken scratches and those rambling things some people write all over their margins. If you use the marks I'm going to show you now you'll be able to mark the hard copy of any document as you go, legibly, so that other people can read it, but more important so that you can read it yourself. Proofreaders' marks are a collection of signs that make up an editing language everyone can read. Remember the Tower of Babel? It was doomed to failure because no one spoke the same language. So proofreaders' marks are standardized to be clear to most people who write and edit.

The proofreaders' marks themselves will show you what sort of problems writers often have in their manuscripts. So, read this section carefully, and when you think you've got a handle on each of the marks, go on to do the exercises that follow.

DELETIONS

Mark	Explanations And Examples	Mark	Correction
	The symbol for "take out," "delete," or "omit" is:	ℐ	
ℐ/	Speak slow, if you speak love		Speak low, if you speak love.
	To know what all makes one tolerant.	/ ℐ	To know all makes one tolerant.
ℐ	None of his friends, like him.		None of his friends like him.

	Use "horns" to indicate remainder is one word:	⌐⌐	
	Come up and see me sor̸metime.	⌐ℐ⌐	Come up and see me sometime.

	Use "lead" mark to delete space:	#	
#ℐ	Con-found all /presents wot eat!	#ℐ	Con-found all presents wot eat!

INSERTIONS

	Mark a caret ⌃ in text, **Letter or symbol in margin**		
	I loaf̸ and invite my soul.	/e	I loafe and invite my soul.
not/	Curfew must‿ring tonight.		Curfew must not ring tonight.

	Never mind her go on talking.	⊙⦔	Never mind her; go on talking.
	Use "horns" to indicate insertion joins another word:	⌐⌐	
	Meet me by moon alone.	/light ⌐⌐	Meet me by moonlight alone.

PUNCTUATION MARKS

A period is so tiny it might get lost: circle it! ⊙

⊙	I never apologize		I never apologize.
	Look-alike comma and apostrophe need "positioning":	⌐ ⸍ ⸝	
⸝	This is Dr. Charles physician. This is Dr. Charles physician.	⌐ ⸍	This is Dr. Charles' physician. This is Dr. Charles, physician.

CHANGES

	Strike out unwanted character(s); show new one(s) in the margin:		
	O! thereby hangs a tale; /	/⊙	O! thereby hangs a tale.
K ≡	/kissing don't last; cookery do!		Kissing don't last; cookery do!
	There is a spirit it/the woods.	/n	There is a spirit in the woods.
/	All the world/s a stage.	not ⌐/	All the world's a stage.
	We are but amused.	/not	We are not amused.
	Nature is usually Wrong.	lc	Nature is usually wrong.

TRANSPOSITIONS

Simple transpositions need simple marking:

⁄tr	'Tis as cheap standing as sitting.		'Tis as cheap sitting as standing.
	There's two to words that bargain.	⁄tr	There's two words to that bargain.
⁄tr	This is the end of the beginning.		This is the beginning of the end.

MISCELLANY

	"Stet" means "let it stand" I've changed my mind:	— — —	stet

stet	We're here because we're here.		We're here because we're here.
	Come away, O human child!	stet	Come away, O human child!
stet rom	Keep yourself to yourself.		Keep yourself *to* yourself.

On the next page you'll find a passage from Shakespeare's play *Hamlet*. There are errors in the original typescript in the left-hand column. I've marked the errors for you and written the corrected copy in the right-hand column so you can see how a marked manuscript looks. As you read through, try to follow the reasons for each mark and review how each mark translates to the corrected copy on the right.

Recap Proofreaders' Marks in Shakespeare Passage

MARK	SYMBOL	MEANING
<u>Enter</u> HAMLET.	ital	set in italics
¶ ∧Ham. To be, or not to be: that is the question:	¶	begin a paragraph
Whether 't is nobler in the mind to suffer	G?	grammar?
The slings and arrows of outrageous fortune	⌐#	close up/ less space/ take out space
Or to take arms against a sea of troubles,	⊃	move right/flush left
And end by opposing them? To die: to sleep:	tr	transpose
No More; and by a sleep to say we end	lc	set in lower case
The heart-ache and the 1000 natural shocks	sp	spell out
That flesh is heir to ∧t is a consummation	⌒	insert comma
Devoutly ✓to ✓be✓wish'd✓To die✓ to sleep;	eq #	equalize space
To sleep: perchance to dream: ay, there's	C	move left/square up
☐ ☐ ☐ ← the rub;		move left–indent 3 ems

197

For in that sleep of death what dreams may / come	‿	move down
When we have shuffled off this mortal coil,	au	author query
Must give us pause. There's the res pect	⌐	close up completely/take out space
That makes calamity of soo long life;	℘	delete

For who would bear the whips and scorns of time,	# /	insert space
The oppressor's wrong, the proud mans contumely	,⋀	insert apostrophe
The pings of disprized love, the law's delay,	/ a	substitute letter
The ns lence of office, and the spurns	═══	straighten type horizontally
That patient merit of the unworthy takes	rom	set in Roman type
When he himself might his quietus make	stet	let it stand
With a bear bodkin who would fardels bear,	?	insert question mark
to grunt and sweat under a weary life,	cap	set in capitals
But that the dread of something death,	after	insert/insert omitted matter

PROOFMARKING TECHNIQUE

1. Use a fine pen.
2. Write (or print) clearly in the margins.
3. Keep marks within the text to a minimum.
4. Every direction is dual: (a) in the margin and (b) in the text.
5. Use strokes in margin both to call attention to and to separate multiple corrections.

Try your skills on the proofmarking exercise that follows.

PROOFMARKING EXERCISE #1

	Example	Problem	Mark(s)
1.	She had earned a Phd along with her M.D.		
2.	The piano as well as the guitar need tuning.		
3.	The student lost their book.		
4.	The storm had the effect of causing millions of dollars in damage.		
5.	We spent the Fall in spain.		
6.	Raoul tried his best, this time that wasn't good enough.		
7.	Due to the fact that we were wondering as to whether it would rain, we stayed home.		
8.	Working harder than ever, this job proved to be too much for him to handle.		
9.	Last summer he walk all the way to Birmingham.		
10.	Depending on the amount of snow we get this winter and whether the towns buy new trucks.		
11.	My income is bigger than my wife.		

12.	A student in accounting would be wise to see their advisor this month.		
13.	My aunt and my mother have wrecked her car.		
14.	The committee has lost their chance to change things.		
15..	You'll have to do this on one's own time.		
16.	The car was blue in color.		
17.	This sentence is flaude with two mispelllings.		
18.	He wonder what these teacher think of him.		
19.	The problem with these cities are leadership.		
20.	He comes into the room and he pulled his gun.		
21.	Seldom have we perused a document so verbose, so ostentatious in phrasing, so burdened with too many words.		
22.	What affect did the movie have on Sheila?		

ANSWER KEY: PROOFMARKING EXERCISE #1

	Abbreviation	Problem	Highlighted Corrections
1.	Ab	**a faulty abbreviation**	**She had earned a Ph.D. along with her M.D.**
2.	Agr See also P/A and	**Agreement problem:** **subject/verb** *or*	**The piano as well as the guitar needs tuning.**
3.	S/V	**pronoun/antecedent**	**The students lost their books.**
4.	Awk	**awkward expression** **or construction**	**The storm had the effect of causing (caused) millions of dollars in damage.**
5.	Cap	**faulty capitalization**	**We spent the fall in Spain.**
6.	CS	**comma splice**	**Raoul tried his best; this time that wasn't good enough.**
7.	DICT	**faulty diction**	Due to the fact that we were wondering as to whether it would rain, we stayed home. We were wondering if it would rain, so we stayed home.
8.	Dgl	**Dangling** **construction**	Working harder than ever, this job **proved to be too much for him to handle.** He was working harder than ever. This job was too much for him to handle.
9.	- ed	**problem with** **final** *-ed*	**Last summer he walked all the way to Birmingham.**
10.	Frag	**fragment**	**We'll get snow blowers, depending on the amount of snow we get this winter and whether the towns buy new trucks.** **If we get enough snow this winter and the towns buy new trucks, we'll get snow blowers.**

11.	‖	problem in parallel form	My income is bigger than my outgo.
12.	P/A	pronoun/antecedent agreement	A student in accounting would be wise to see his/her advisor this month.
13.	Pron	problem with pronoun	My aunt and my mother have wrecked Mom's car.
14.			The committee has lost its chance to change things.
15.			You'll have to do this on your own time.
16.	Rep	unnecessary repetition	The car was blue in color.
17.	Sp	spelling error	This sentence is flawed with two misspellings.
18.	- s	problem with final –s	He wonders what these teachers think of him.
19.	S/V	subject/verb agreement	The problem with these cities is leadership.
20.	T	verb tense problem	He comes into the room and he pulls his gun.
21.	Wdy	wordy	Seldom have we perused a document so verbose, so ostentatious in phrasing, so burdened with too many words. We've never seen anything so wordy.
22.	WW	wrong word	What effect did the movie have on Sheila?

PROOFREADING RECAP

- Print it out
- Let it cool
- Read it out loud
- Cover everything past the line you're reading with a blank sheet of paper
- Check all names and titles
- Check all small words—or and of are often interchanged, so are it and is
- Check the math
- Check spacing between words and between paragraphs
- Check for extra letters and repeated words
- Check for missing words
- Check for incomplete sets of parentheses and quotation marks
- Check for ie and ei spelling mix-ups
- Check for mistyped numbers

For detailed proofreading advice, check these websites:

http://webnz.com/checkers/proof2.html

http://www.writing.ku.edu/students/guides.html

MISSION IMPOSSIBLE PROOFREADING

This fascinating essay on the importance of proofreading was written by an extremely diabolical student. There are 58 mistakes in   the exercise. How many can you find?

Is proofreading important?

Proofreading is very important. Profreading is the final step in the writing proces that makes a document perfect.
Every writer needs profreading to successfuly finish a letter, an contract, or a book. For profesional or private purposes, profreading is the ultimatte step in the writing proces. There is non such thing as writing a perfect document from scratsch. Writing is a proces that contain the following: praewriting (100/o)*, rugh draft (15%), rewising (400/o), editing (300/o) and piofreading (100/o). Profreading just takes little time, but is the finally step in the process befor the document go to the readers. Profreading is a marketing process. Imagine how difficouh it would be four a CEO if he gived a presentation using slides with tipos in them. Before Al Gore gived a presentation, he gives the pictures to at least four diferent people to proofread it.
In fact profreading just take you as little as five @nuies! Imagine'y'ou would invest two houres on an important presentation or on an nice letter and the result would be much destroyed by just a couple of tipos. Remember you just need five minutes to make your hard work perfekt! Profreading helped me a lot. My documents became much more profesional! Do as I did! Profread. If you didn't do it, you vast your valuable time. Spend aditional five minutes on profreading!
*necessary time in % of the total writing time.

ANSWER KEY: MISSION IMPOSSIBLE PROOFREADING

<u>Is proofreading important?</u>

Proofreading is very important. **Profre**ading is the final step in the writing **proces** that makes a document perfect. Every writer needs **profreading** to **successfuly** finish a letter, **an** contract, or a book. For **profesional** or private purposes, **profreading** is the **ultimatte** step in the writing **proces**. There is **non** such thing as writing a perfect document from **scratsch**.

Writing is a **proces** that **contain** the following: **praewriting** (100/o)*, **rugh** draft (15%), **rewising** (400/o), editing (300/o) and **piofreading** (100/o). **Profreading** just takes __ little time, but is the **finally** step in the process **befor** the document **go** to the readers.

Profreading is a marketing process. Imagine how **difficouh** it would be **four** a CEO if he **gived** a presentation using slides with **tipos** in them. Before Al Gore **gived** a presentation, he gives the pictures to at least four **diferent** people to proofread **it**.

In fact_ **profreading** just **take** you as **little** as five **@nuies**! **Imagine'y'ou would** invest two **houres** on an important presentation or on **an** nice letter and the result **would be much** destroyed by just a couple of **tipos**. Remember you just need five minutes to make your hard work **perfekt**! **Profreading** helped me a lot. My documents became much more **profesional**! Do as I **did**! **Profread**. If you **didn't** do it, you **vast** your valuable time. Spend__ **aditional** five minutes on **profreading**!

*necessary time in % of the total writing time **(percentages add up to 115%)**

Please write your journal entry for Chapter 16 **NOW.** For instructions, see Page 7.

LAST PAGE

If you've survived all the exercises in this book and all the Internet exercises, hints and quizzes, you're on your way to becoming an excellent business writer. You've knocked down a few barriers and gotten some confidence in your ability to write.

It took me thirty-five years to learn how to write well and there isn't a day that goes by that I don't learn how to write better. The same is true for you. The thing that separates good writers from the rest of the world is that good writers have the courage to get up every day and practice. Even a paragraph a day will make the difference.

I've enjoyed writing for you, and I hope you've enjoyed working with what I've written. Writing has always been my passport to the world. I hope it serves an equally valuable purpose in your life.

K. T. Maclay

INDEX

TRAINING SESSIONS MAKE HOUSECALLS

Business Writing to Go brings instructors to your office or conference room to work with you at *your* pace and on *your* schedule. Courses run from five to twelve sessions concentrating specifically on material you write on the job.

"Both my bosses still comment on how much my writing has improved. They love that I get straight to the point. They have so much faith in my abilities that they let me do the final edit of press releases before they go out."

> Anne Hammel
> Public Relations Associate
> National Multiple Sclerosis Society

Executive Writing Workshops are one-day, group sessions designed as hands-on writing experiences for people who need to communicate effectively with clients, staff, instructors, or colleagues.

A recent report by the National Commission on Writing for America's Families, Schools and Colleges indicates businesses spend more than $3.1 billion annually in remedial training to improve the language and writing of employees. Executive Writing Workshops help your business compete with those who train their people.

"As a professional speaker and writer, and as a teacher, I have the greatest respect for K.T. Maclay's creative methods of teaching speaking and writing, in print and in the classroom. Watching K.T. teach, I was deeply impressed with how she brought out the best in every one of her students. They were charmed, perhaps they were mesmerized, they certainly changed before my eyes, and they learned a lot."

> Mary Campbell Gallagher, J. D., Ph. D.
> President, Gallagher Law & Essay Training Schools

"I learned skills I didn't know I needed. Everyone at every level should take this course."

> Nikita Ovietsky.
> President, Cogitech, Inc.

E-mail me at ktmaclay@gmail.com for up-to-the-minute information.

ABOUT THE AUTHOR

K. T. Maclay has been a master communications trainer since 1992. Her clients include individuals and groups at Merrill Lynch, Goldman Sachs, National Public Radio USA, Deloitte and Touche, Johnson and Johnson, American Express, L'Oreal USA, OppenheimerFunds, Avon, Con Edison and CitiCards.

She works with people who want to write clear documents confidently and coaches writers who have problems with procrastination, wordiness, time pressure or getting results.

Ms. Maclay's **Business Writing To Go** and **Executive Writing Skills** workshops cover tactics that enable participants to begin projects immediately, strategies that help reduce stress, guidelines that indicate exactly where to begin and templates that demonstrate how to finish.

The communications courses she instructs include questions that encourage students to focus on their audience and instill innovative concepts for writing documents people read and remember. Inventive projects and homework assignments help participants in her workshops put their skills into practice in their everyday writing.

K. T. Maclay is the author of four non-fiction books two of which have become Literary Guild selections. **Business Writing, Period.**, the most recent of these books, was designed to accompany Ms. Maclay's courses, workshops and seminars. It provides hands-on, no-nonsense writing experience for anyone who needs to communicate effectively with clients, staff, instructors, colleagues and customers.

Before devoting herself to training, Ms. Maclay spent more than two decades in the corporate world writing and producing projects for Revlon, J. P. Stevens, Goodson-Todman Productions, NBC, ABC, and J. Walter Thompson.

Ms. Maclay speaks two languages in addition to English. She is a student of the psychology of language, of how the brain works and of how human beings learn. Her innovative techniques and dynamic teaching methods have been successfully used with students from São Paulo to Dusseldorf.

She is a member of the Authors Guild and holds a Cambridge certificate in teaching English as a foreign language (CT E F L A.)

YOUR NOTES HERE

YOUR NOTES HERE

www.ingramcontent.com/pod-product-compliance
Lightning Source LLC
Chambersburg PA
CBHW080540220326
41599CB00032B/6328